NELSON MANDELA

A LIFE IN PHOTOGRAPHS

Created by David Elliot Cohen
Text by John D. Battersby

Includes Six Historic Mandela Speeches

STERLING

New York / London
www.sterlingpublishing.com

STERLING and the distinctive Sterling logo are registered
trademarks of Sterling Publishing Co., Inc.

10 9 8 7 6 5 4 3 2 1

Published by Sterling Publishing Co., Inc.
387 Park Avenue South, New York, NY 10016
© 2009 by Western Arts Management, Tiburon CA USA

Distributed in Canada by Sterling Publishing Co.
c/o Canadian Manda Group
165 Dufferin Street
Toronto, Ontario, Canada M6K 3H6

Distributed in the United Kingdom by
GMC Distribution Services,
Castle Place, 166 High Street, Lewes,
East Sussex, England BN7 1XU

Distributed in Australia by
Capricorn Link (Australia) Pty. Ltd.,
P.O. Box 704,Windsor, NSW 2756, Australia

Printed in Canada
All rights reserved

Designed by Peter Truskier and David Elliot Cohen
Production by Peter Truskier, Premedia Systems, Inc.

Sterling ISBN: 978-1-4027-7707-3

FOR INFORMATION about custom editions, special sales,
and premium and corporate purchases, please contact the
Sterling Special Sales Department at 800-805-5489 or
specialsales@sterlingpublishing.com.

YOUR COMMENTS WELCOME:
editor.whatmatters@gmail.com

▶ Nelson Mandela, Johannesburg,
South Africa, April 1, 2004

Photograph by Jehad Nga

FOREWORD

By John D. Battersby

When you are in the presence of a truly great person such as Nelson Mandela, there is no need to analyze what greatness is, nor to work out how he came to be so great.

Being in Mandela's presence is akin to listening to a very good orchestra with a very good conductor playing Beethoven's Fifth Symphony. He creates a magical environment that accommodates and encourages complete expression of one's humanity.

I consider myself very privileged to have known Mandela as a journalist, as a South African, and as a human being. I interviewed him on many occasions as a foreign correspondent, as a South African newspaper editor, and as a political editor. At least six of these interviews were major hours-long discussions and there were many smaller interviews, encounters at state banquets, meet-ups on the election trail, and grip-and-grins with the many celebrities who made the long pilgrimage to meet him.

But there is one interview that stands above all the rest. It took place nearly a year after Mandela stepped down as president, when I was editor of the

◄ **MIND, BODY, AND SPIRIT:** Nelson Mandela, a keen amateur boxer in his youth, trains in the 1950s. "I did not enjoy the violence of boxing so much as the science of it," he said. Mandela found that boxing was an outlet for the stress of waging the anti-apartheid struggle. "After a strenuous workout," he said, "I felt both mentally and physically lighter." Boxing was part of a lifelong program of physical exercise that Mandela saw as an integral part of the discipline essential to meet the rigors of a life in politics and in prison.

Johannesburg newspaper the *Sunday Independent*. I had noticed that during the preceding several months, Mandela had become more philosophical and introspective in his public remarks, and I asked if I could speak with him, on the record, about what he would like his legacy to be. He agreed. He was eighty-two at the time.

I always felt that there was something more to Mandela's goals than achieving a political victory over apartheid and its rulers, although that was certainly a monumental achievement. I felt he had a higher goal: to persuade an entire nation to come around to his innate belief in a broader humanity based on service to the community and the acknowledgment of others' needs and well-being as the basis for one's own existence.

Although a much-abused word these days, Mandela's goal embodies what is known in African culture as *ubuntu*. It is a philosophy that underlies the warm relationship between Mandela and his fellow Nobel Peace Prize laureate Archbishop Desmond Tutu, and perhaps it was Tutu who described *ubuntu* best in his 1999 book, *No Future Without Forgiveness*:

> A person with Ubuntu is open and available to others, affirming of others, does not feel threatened that others are able and good, for he or she has a proper self-assurance that comes from knowing that he or she belongs in a greater whole and is diminished when others are humiliated or diminished, when others are tortured or oppressed.

How did Mandela, a very angry young man by any measure, achieve this level of *ubuntu*? In the "summing-up interview" I conducted with Mandela, which was published in the *Christian Science Monitor* in 2000, he identified several processes in his life that had changed him and made it possible for him to achieve the goals he had set for himself. Most of these processes, he said, took place during his twenty-seven years in prison.

Mandela's biographer Anthony Sampson, who knew Mandela before he went to prison in 1963, noted the remarkable transformation in the man who emerged from jail, compared with the impulsive, quick-tempered activist whom Sampson knew in the late 1950s.

Mandela conceded to me that in those days the loss of dignity and the humiliation he suffered under apartheid sparked angry reactions rather than rational analysis and discussion. But in prison, Mandela said, he had time to think and to listen to the stories of those around him.

He had time to think about those people in his life who had helped him, and how he had often failed to acknowledge their generosity and compassion. After his release from prison, he often went out of his way to publicly acknowledge the generosity of others.

He had time to read the biographies of other famous people whose lives had changed humanity for the better. In doing so, he learned that difficulties and disaster destroyed some people but positively transformed others. He said the people he admired most were those who were able to turn disaster into success.

I always felt that there was something more to Mandela's goals than achieving a political victory over apartheid and its rulers.

He also told me that the prison experience had taught him to respect even the most ordinary people, and that he was always surprised how wrong one could be in judging people before speaking to them and finding out their unique story.

Finally, he told me that a true leader was one who thought about the poor twenty-four hours a day and who knew in his or her heart that poverty was the biggest threat to society.

When U.S. President Bill Clinton paid a state visit to South Africa in 1998, he went with Mandela—with whom he had a natural rapport and developed a close friendship—to Robben Island to visit the jail cell where Mandela spent nineteen years of his life, virtually his whole middle age.

In a 2004 interview with the *Guardian* before the publication of his autobiography, *My Life*, Clinton said Mandela had counseled him and stood by him throughout the Monica Lewinsky affair and had helped him save his marriage and get past the effects of the scandal.

Clinton said that while they were alone together in his old cell, Mandela had told him that he forgave his oppressors because if he had not, it would have destroyed him.

Mandela said that his jailers had taken the best years of his life, that he didn't get to see his children grow up. They had abused him mentally and physically, and they destroyed his marriage. But despite this, Mandela would not let himself live in anger, because he would not let them take his mind and his heart.

Mandela insists that if you want to achieve your goals in life, you cannot afford to engage in anger and you cannot waste your life fighting with the enemy. You rather want to create the conditions in which you can move everybody toward your goals.

And that is exactly what he did in 1995, when he engineered a massive shift in white public opinion by throwing his presidential weight behind the overwhelmingly white national rugby team, a potent symbol of the former apartheid regime. It was a watershed moment for South Africa. The Springboks won the World Cup of rugby, but—as John Carlin describes in his brilliant book *Playing the Enemy*—Mandela won the country.

▼ **FOLLOWING PAGE:** In December 1951, thirty-three-year-old Mandela was a leading member of the ANC Youth League, which he had helped found in 1944. Ruth First was a journalist, an active ANC member, and the wife of ANC stalwart and South African Communist Party chief Joe Slovo. Here Mandela and First (behind him, in sunglasses) are seen following the crucial ANC conference in the city of Bloemfontein that approved the Defiance Campaign against unjust laws. The Defiance Campaign was a seminal event that led to a total of 8,500 arrests and raised international awareness of the growing apartheid crisis.

Photograph from *Drum* magazine

▶ **TRADITIONAL DRESS:** In this 1962 photograph, Mandela wears the authentic beaded necklace and toga-like robes of the Thembu clan, one of the clans that make up the Xhosa tribe. This portrait was taken while Mandela was on the run from the apartheid police in 1961 and 1962. Mandela, perhaps more than any other South African leader, succeeded in maintaining pride in his tribal upbringing as the son of a minor Xhosa chief while at the same time embracing modern urban life and all that it had to offer. He always retained his strong links with his tribal birthplace in the Transkei and maintained a home there.

NO EASY WALK TO FREEDOM

September 21, 1953

Nelson Mandela wrote this address upon being elected president of the African National Congress in the Transvaal[1] region in 1953. The South African government had banned him from speaking in public, so the address was read on his behalf at the ANC's Transvaal conference.[2]

Since 1912[3] and year after year thereafter, in their homes and local areas, in provincial and national gatherings, on trains and buses, in the factories and on the farms, in cities, villages, shantytowns, schools, and prisons, the African people have discussed the shameful misdeeds of those who rule the country. Year after year, they have raised their voices in condemnation of the grinding poverty of the people, the low wages, the acute shortage of land, the inhuman exploitation, and the whole policy of white domination. But instead of more freedom, repression began to grow in volume and intensity, and it seemed that all their sacrifices would end up in smoke and dust. Today the entire country knows that their labors were not in vain. For a new spirit and new ideas have gripped our people. Today the people speak the language of action: there is a mighty awakening among the men and women of our country, and the year

[1] The Transvaal is an area of northern South Africa that made up most of the independent Boer South African Republic. After the Boer War of 1899–1902, it became the Transvaal Colony, one of the founding provinces of the Union of South Africa. The region now comprises the modern provinces of Gauteng, Limpopo, and Mpumalanga as well as part of the North West Province. The Transvaal contains South Africa's capital, Pretoria, and its largest city, Johannesburg. Despite its official disintegration, the Transvaal is still a commonly used geographical term and retains its historical significance.

[2] Certain sections of this speech, indicated by ellipses [...], have been omitted. Footnotes have been added to explain certain historical references, and words have been added in brackets [ ] for the same purpose. Spelling and punctuation have been Americanized. This speech, in its entirety, and many others by Mandela, can be found at www.anc.org.za, the website of the African National Congress.

[3] In 1912, the African National Congress was formed in Bloemfontein, South Africa.

1952 stands out as the year of this upsurge of national consciousness.

In June 1952, the African National Congress and the South African Indian Congress, bearing in mind their responsibility as the representatives of the downtrodden and oppressed people of South Africa, took the plunge and launched the Campaign for the Defiance of the Unjust Laws. Starting off in Port Elizabeth in the early hours of June 26 and with only 33 defiers in action, and then in Johannesburg in the afternoon of the same day with 166 defiers, it spread throughout the country like wildfire. Factory and office workers, doctors, lawyers, teachers, students, and the clergy; Africans, Coloreds, Indians, and Europeans; old and young, all rallied to the national call and defied the pass laws and the curfew and the railway apartheid regulations. At the end of the year, more than 8,000 people of all races had defied. The campaign called for immediate and heavy sacrifices. Workers lost their jobs; chiefs and teachers were expelled from the service; doctors, lawyers, and businessmen gave up their practices and businesses, and [instead] elected to go to jail.

Defiance was a step of great political significance. It released strong social forces which affected thousands of our countrymen. It was an effective way of getting the masses to function politically, a powerful method of voicing our indignation against the reactionary policies of the government. It was one of the best ways of exerting pressure on the government and extremely dangerous to the stability and security of the state. It inspired and aroused our people from a conquered and servile community of "yes-men" to a militant and uncompromising band of comrades-in-arms. The entire country was transformed into battle zones where the forces of liberation were locked up in immortal conflict against those of reaction and evil. Our flag flew in every battlefield and thousands of our countrymen rallied around it. We held the initiative and the forces of freedom were advancing on all fronts…

Today we meet under totally different conditions. By the end of July last year, the Campaign had reached a stage where it had to be suppressed by the government or it would impose its own policies on the country.

The government launched its reactionary offensive and struck at us. Between July last year and August this year, forty-seven leading members from both Congresses[4] in Johannesburg, Port Elizabeth, and Kimberley were arrested, tried, and convicted for launching the Defiance Campaign and given suspended sentences ranging from three months to two years on condition that they did not again participate in the defiance of the unjust laws. In November last year, a proclamation was passed which prohibited meetings of more than ten Africans and made it an offense for any person to call upon an African to defy [the unjust laws]. Contravention of this proclamation carried a penalty of three years or a fine of three hundred pounds. In March this year the government passed the so-called Public Safety Act, which empowered it to declare a state of emergency and to create conditions which would permit the most

Defiance was a powerful method of voicing our indignation against the reactionary policies of the government.

ruthless and pitiless methods of suppressing our movement. Almost simultaneously, the Criminal Laws Amendment Act was passed which provided heavy penalties for those convicted of Defiance [Campaign] offenses. This act also made provision for the whipping of defiers including women. It was under this act that Mr. Arthur Matlala, who was the local [leader] of the Central Branch during the Defiance Campaign, was convicted and sentenced to twelve months [of] hard labor plus eight strokes [of the whip]…

The Congresses realized that these measures created a new situation which did not prevail when the [Defiance] Campaign was launched in June 1952. The tide of defiance was bound to recede, and we were forced to pause and to take stock of the new situation. We had to analyze the dangers that faced us, formulate plans to overcome them, and evolve new plans of political struggle. A political movement must keep in touch with reality and the prevailing conditions. Long speeches, the shaking of fists, the banging of tables, and

[4] The African National Congress and the South African Indian Congress.

strongly worded resolutions out of touch with the objective conditions do not bring about mass action and can do a great deal of harm to the organization and the struggle we serve. The masses had to be prepared and made ready for new forms of political struggle. We had to recuperate our strength and muster our forces for another and more powerful offensive against the enemy. To have gone ahead blindly as if nothing had happened would have been suicidal and stupid…

The Defiance Campaign, together with its thrills and adventures, has receded. The old methods of bringing about mass action through public mass meetings, press statements, and leaflets calling upon the people to go to action have become extremely dangerous and difficult to use effectively. The authorities will not easily permit a meeting called under the auspices of the ANC, few newspapers will publish statements openly criticizing the policies of the government, and there is hardly a single printing press which will agree to print leaflets calling upon workers to embark on industrial action for fear of prosecution under the Suppression of Communism Act and similar measures. These developments require the evolution of new forms of political struggle which will make it reasonable for us to strive for action on a higher level than the Defiance Campaign.

The government, alarmed at the indomitable upsurge of national consciousness, is doing everything in its power to crush our movement by removing the genuine representatives of the people from the organizations. According to a statement made by Swart[5] in Parliament on the 18th September 1953, there

[5] Charles Robberts Swart (1894–1982), a minister of justice who subsequently became the last governor-general of the Union of South Africa, from 1960 to 1961, and then served as the first state president of the Republic of South Africa, from 1961 to 1967.

are thirty-three trade union officials and eighty-nine other people who have been served with notices in terms of the Suppression of Communism Act. This does not include that formidable array of freedom fighters who have been named and blacklisted under the Suppression of Communism Act and those who have been banned under the Riotous Assemblies Act.

The living conditions of the people, already extremely difficult, are becoming unbearable.

Meanwhile, the living conditions of the people, already extremely difficult, are steadily worsening and becoming unbearable. The purchasing power of the masses is progressively declining and the cost of living is rocketing. Bread is now dearer than it was two months ago. The cost of milk, meat, and vegetables is beyond the pockets of the average family, and many of our people cannot afford them. The people are too poor to have enough food to feed their families and children. They cannot afford sufficient clothing, housing, and medical care. They are denied the right to security in the event of unemployment, sickness, disability, old age; and where these exist, they are of an extremely inferior and useless nature.

Because of lack of proper medical amenities, our people are ravaged by such dreaded diseases as tuberculosis, venereal disease, leprosy, pellagra; and infantile mortality is very high. The recent state budget made provision for the increase of the cost-of-living allowances for Europeans, and not a word was said about the poorest and most hard-hit section of the population—the African people. The insane policies of the government which have brought about an explosive situation in the country have definitely scared away foreign capital from South Africa, and the financial crisis through which the country is now passing is forcing many industrial and business concerns to close down, to retrench their staffs, and unemployment is growing every day.

The farm laborers are in a particularly dire plight. You will perhaps recall the investigations and exposures of the semi-slave conditions on the Bethal

▲ **AT THE CROSSROADS:** In the 1950s and 1960s, Mandela's tailored suits, high-parted hair, and strong Xhosa features wove the strands of urbane elegance and royal tribal lineage into an alluring public figure.

farms made in 1948 by the Reverend Michael Scott[6] and a *Guardian* correspondent; by the *Drum*[7] last year; and [by] the *Advance* in April this year. You will recall how human beings, wearing only sacks with holes for their heads and arms, never given enough food to eat, slept on cement floors on cold nights with only their sacks to cover their shivering bodies. You will remember how they are woken up as early as 4 a.m. and taken to work in the fields with the *indunas*[8] *sjambokking*[9] those who tried to straighten their backs, who felt weak and dropped down because of hunger and sheer exhaustion. You will also recall the story of human beings toiling pathetically from the early hours of the morning till sunset, fed only on mealie meal[10] served on filthy sacks spread on the ground and eating with their dirty hands. People falling ill and never once being given medical attention. You will also recall the revolting story of a farmer who was convicted for tying a laborer by his feet from a tree and [having] him flogged to death, pouring boiling water into his mouth whenever he cried for water. These things which have long vanished from many parts of the world still flourish in [South Africa] today. None will deny that they constitute a serious challenge to Congress, and we are duty-bound to find an effective remedy for these obnoxious practices.

The government has introduced in Parliament the Native Labor (Settlement of Disputes) Bill and the Bantu Education Bill. Speaking on the labor bill, the Minister of Labor, Ben Schoeman, openly stated that the aim of this wicked measure is to bleed African trade unions to death. By forbidding strikes and lockouts, it deprives Africans of the one weapon the workers have to improve their position. The aim of the measure is to destroy the present African trade unions, which are controlled by the workers themselves and which fight for

[6] A British anti-apartheid activist and leading proponent of Namibian independence.

[7] A historically important African publication in South Africa. Several photos in this book were taken by *Drum* photographers, including Jurgen Schadenberg, Alf Khumalo, and Peter Magubane.

[8] A Zulu title meaning, in this case, "headman."

[9] Whipping with a *sjambok*, a whip traditionally made from hippopotamus or rhino hide, later made from plastic and closely associated with apartheid rule in the same way as the bullwhip is symbolically associated with slavery in the United States.

[10] A staple food made from ground maize.

the improvement of their working conditions, in return for a Central Native Labor Board controlled by the government, which will be used to frustrate the legitimate aspirations of the African worker. The Minister of Native Affairs, Verwoerd,[11] has also been brutally clear in explaining the objects of the Bantu Education Bill. According to him, the aim of this law is to teach our children that Africans are inferior to Europeans. African education would be taken out of the hands of people who taught equality between black and white. When this bill becomes law, it will not be the parents, but the Department of Native Affairs, which will decide whether an African child should receive higher or other education. It might well be that the children of those who criticize the government and who fight its policies will almost certainly be taught how to drill rocks in the mines and how to plow potatoes on the farms of Bethal. High education might well be the privilege of those children whose families have a tradition of collaboration with the ruling circles.

The attitude of the government to us is: Let's beat them down with guns and batons. Let's drown the whole country in blood if only there is the slightest chance of preserving white supremacy.

The attitude of the [African National] Congress on these bills is very clear and unequivocal. Congress totally rejects both bills without reservation. The last provincial conference strongly condemned the then proposed labor bill as a measure designed to rob the African workers of the universal right of free trade unionism and to undermine and destroy the existing African trade unions. Conference further

[11] Hendrik Verwoerd (1901–66), called the "architect of apartheid" for his role in the implementation of apartheid policy as minister of native affairs during the early 1950s. He later became prime minister of South Africa and served from 1958 until his assassination in 1966.

called upon the African workers to boycott and defy the application of this sinister scheme which was calculated to further the exploitation of the African worker. To accept a measure of this nature even in a qualified manner would be a betrayal of the toiling masses. At a time when every genuine Congressite should fight unreservedly for the recognition of African trade unions and the realization of the principle that everyone has the right to form and to join trade unions for the protection of his interests, we declare our firm belief in the principles enunciated in the Universal Declaration of Human Rights: that everyone has the right to education; that education shall be directed to the full development of human personality and to the strengthening of respect for human rights and fundamental freedoms; [that education] shall promote understanding, tolerance, and friendship among the nations, racial or religious groups, and shall further the activities of the United Nations for the maintenance of peace; that parents have the right to choose the kind of education that shall be given to their children.

The cumulative effect of all these measures is to prop up and perpetuate the artificial and decaying policy of the supremacy of the white men. The attitude of the government to us is: "Let's beat them down with guns and batons and trample them under our feet. We must be ready to drown the whole country in blood if only there is the slightest chance of preserving white supremacy."

But there is nothing inherently superior about the *herrenvolk*[12] idea of the supremacy of the whites. In China, India, Indonesia, and Korea, American, British, Dutch, and French imperialism, based on the concept of the supremacy of Europeans over Asians, has been completely and perfectly exploded. In Malaya[13] and Indochina[14], British and French imperialisms are being shaken to their foundations by powerful and revolutionary national

[12] A concept, often associated with Nazi ideology, which contends that the Teutonic or Nordic branch of the "Aryan race" is the ideal "master race."

[13] A group of small states on the Malay Peninsula that were colonized by the British until the mid-twentieth century.

[14] An area of Southeast Asia that lies east of India and south of China. Now includes the nations of Vietnam, Cambodia, Laos, and Myanmar.

liberation movements. In Africa, there are approximately 190 million Africans as against 4 million Europeans. The entire continent is seething with discontent, and already there are powerful revolutionary eruptions in the Gold Coast,[15] Nigeria, Tunisia, Kenya, the Rhodesias,[16] and South Africa. The oppressed people and the oppressors are at loggerheads. The day of reckoning between the forces of freedom and those of reaction is not very far off. I have not the slightest doubt that when that day comes, truth and justice will prevail.

The intensification of repressions and the extensive use of the bans is designed to immobilize every active worker and to check the national liberation movement. But gone forever are the days when harsh and wicked laws provided the oppressors with years of peace and quiet. The racial policies of the government have pricked the conscience of all men of goodwill and have aroused their deepest indignation. The feelings of the oppressed people have never been more bitter. If the ruling circles seek to maintain their position by such inhuman methods, then a clash between the forces of freedom and those of reaction is certain. The grave plight of the people compels them to resist to the death the stinking policies of the gangsters that rule our country.

But in spite of all the difficulties outlined above, we have won important victories. The general political level of the people has been considerably raised, and they are now more conscious of their strength. Action has become the language of the day. The ties between the working people and the [African National] Congress have been greatly strengthened. This is a development of the highest importance because in a country such as ours, a political organization that does not receive the support of the workers is in fact paralyzed on the very ground on which it has chosen to wage battle. Leaders of trade union organizations are at the same time important officials of the provincial and local branches of the ANC. In the past we talked of the African, Indian, and Colored struggles. Though certain individuals raised the question of a united

[15] Now Ghana.

[16] Now Zimbabwe and Zambia.

front of all the oppressed groups, the various non-European organizations stood miles apart from one another, and the efforts of those for coordination and unity were like a voice crying in the wilderness; and it seemed that the day would never dawn when the oppressed people would stand and fight together, shoulder to shoulder, against a common enemy. Today we talk of the struggle of the oppressed people, which, though it is waged through their respective autonomous organizations, is gravitating towards one central command…

Our immediate task is to consolidate these victories, to preserve our organizations and to muster our forces for the resumption of the offensive… From now on the activity of Congressites must not be confined to speeches and resolutions. Their activities must find expression in wide-scale work among the masses, work which will enable them to make the greatest possible contact with the working people. You must protect and defend your trade unions. If you are not allowed to have your meetings publicly, then you must hold them over your machines in the factories, on the trains and buses as you travel home. You must have them in your villages and shantytowns. You must make every home, every shack, and every mud structure where our people live, a branch of the trade union movement and never surrender.

You must defend the right of African parents to decide the kind of education that shall be given to their children. Teach the children that Africans are not one iota inferior to Europeans. Establish your own community schools where the right kind of education will be given to our children. If it becomes

> You must defend the right of African parents to decide the kind of education that shall be given to their children. Teach the children that Africans are not one iota inferior to Europeans.

dangerous or impossible to have these alternative schools, then again you must make every home, every shack or rickety structure a center of learning for our children. Never surrender to the inhuman and barbaric theories of Verwoerd…

There is no easy walk to freedom anywhere, and many of us will have to pass through the valley of the shadow again and again before we reach the mountaintops of our desires.

Here in South Africa, as in many parts of the world, a revolution is maturing: it is the profound desire, the determination, and the urge of the overwhelming majority of the country to destroy forever the shackles of oppression that condemn them to servitude and slavery. To overthrow oppression has been sanctioned by humanity and is the highest aspiration of every free man. If elements in our organization seek to impede the realization of this lofty purpose, then these people have placed themselves outside the organization and must be put out of action before they do more harm. To do otherwise would be a crime and a serious neglect of duty. We must rid ourselves of such elements and give our organization the striking power of a real militant mass organization.

Kotane, Marks, Bopape, Tloome,[17] and I have been banned from attending gatherings, and we cannot join and counsel with you on the serious problems that are facing our country. We have been banned because we champion the freedom of the oppressed people of our country and because we have consistently fought against the policy of racial discrimination in favor of a policy which accords fundamental human rights to all, irrespective of race, color, sex, or language. We are exiled from our own people, for we have uncompromisingly resisted the efforts of imperialist America and her satellites

[17] Moses Kotane, J. B. Marks, David Wilcox Hlahane Bopape, and Daniel Tloome were political activists at the time.

to drag the world into the rule of violence and brutal force, into the rule of the napalm, hydrogen, and the cobalt bombs where millions of people will be wiped out to satisfy the criminal and greedy appetites of the imperial powers. We have been gagged because we have emphatically and openly condemned the criminal attacks by the imperialists against the people of Malaya, Vietnam, Indonesia, Tunisia, and Tanganyika and called upon our people to identify themselves unreservedly with the cause of world peace and to fight against the war policies of America and her satellites. We are being shadowed, hounded, and trailed because we fearlessly voiced our horror and indignation at the slaughter of the people of Korea and Kenya. The massacre of the Kenya[n] people by Britain has aroused worldwide indignation and protest. Children are being burnt alive, women are raped, tortured, whipped and boiling water poured on their breasts to force confessions from them that Jomo Kenyatta had administered the Mau Mau oath to them. Men are being castrated and shot dead. In the Kikuyu country there are some villages in which the population has been completely wiped out. We are prisoners in our own country because we dared to raise our voices against these horrible atrocities and because we expressed our solidarity with the cause of the Kenya[n] people.

You can see that "there is no easy walk to freedom anywhere, and many of us will have to pass through the valley of the shadow (of death) again and again before we reach the mountaintops of our desires."[18]

"Dangers and difficulties have not deterred us in the past; they will not frighten us now. But we must be prepared for them like men in business, who do not waste energy in vain talk and idle action. The way of preparation (for action) lies in our rooting out all impurity and indiscipline from our organization and making it the bright and shining instrument that will cleave its way to (Africa's) freedom."

[18] Although he includes no attribution in the speech, Mandela quotes here from a 1939 article, "From Lucknow to Tripoli," by Indian Prime Minister Jawaharlal Nehru, reprinted in a compilation of his articles under the title *The Unity of India: Collected Writings 1937–40* (Lindsay Drummond, 1942) and in *Selected Works of Jawaharlal Nehru*, volume 9 (Orient Longman, 1976). Nehru originally wrote: "There is no easy walk-over to freedom anywhere, and many of us will have to pass through the valley of the shadow again and again before we reach the mountain-tops of our desire." Added words in parentheses are Mandela's.

▲ **MANDELA'S FIRST FAMILY:** Mandela married his first wife, Evelyn Ntoko Mase, on July 14, 1944. The couple had four children: a daughter, Makaziwe (Maki), who died when she was nine months old; a second daughter with the same name; a son, Thembekile (Thembi), who died in a road accident in 1969; and a second son, Makgatho, who died from AIDS in 2005. Mandela publicly discussed the cause of Makgotho's death in a bid to break the taboo surrounding AIDS in South Africa. Evelyn, a devout Jehovah's Witness who had little taste for revolution, separated from Nelson in 1955, and the couple divorced in March 1958. Three months later, Mandela married his second wife, Winnie.

◀ **MANDELA & TAMBO, ATTORNEYS:** In 1952, Mandela and his lifelong friend and colleague, Oliver Tambo, set up the country's first black legal practice in Johannesburg. Mandela had moved from the Xhosa heartland in Transkei to Johannesburg in 1941 to escape an arranged marriage. Tambo, who was a founding member of the ANC Youth League with Mandela, eventually went on to become president of the ANC in exile. Even after Mandela was freed and became an international icon in 1990, he insisted that Tambo retain the title of ANC president.

▲ DEFIANCE TRIAL: The 1952 Defiance Campaign targeted laws that forced black South Africans to carry identity documents (or "passes"), enforced residential segregation, denied blacks the vote, and branded resistance to apartheid as communism. The civil disobedience campaign, conducted in the tradition of Mahatma Gandhi's philosophy of passive resistance (*satyagraha*), shook the apartheid establishment, which responded with series of arrests and trials. Here, Mandela surveys newspaper coverage with then-ANC leader J. S. Moroka (left) and Yusuf Dadoo, who was head of the affiliated South African Indian Congress and a leader of the South African Communist Party. The Communist Party, which backed the anti-apartheid struggle, was a close ally of the ANC throughout the struggle and still plays a key role in its leadership. Mandela cooperated closely with communist leaders such as Joe Slovo (1926–95) to reach a compromise with the apartheid government over power sharing with black South Africans.

Photograph by Jurgen Schadeberg

▶ MANDELA (CENTER) is flanked by Walter Sisulu (left) and Nthato Harrison Motlana, co-leaders of the ANC Youth League, which played a central role in the seminal 1952 Defiance Campaign against unjust laws. Sisulu, who was a few years older than Mandela, was a lifelong friend and mentor; Motlana, a medical doctor, twice stood trial with Mandela and became a prominent anti-apartheid activist.

Women
played a frontline
role in protesting
racist laws in
South Africa.

▶ **ADDRESSING HIS CLIENTS:** Mandela addresses a group of women arrested for protesting racist education laws in 1955. Mandela, who represented the twenty-one women in court, is briefing them on defense procedures. The women were charged with disturbing the public peace by shouting, making noises, and quarreling. Women traditionally played a frontline role in protesting racist laws in South Africa. These women's actions were part of a protest against the Bantu Education Act, a cornerstone of apartheid law that ensured not only that blacks received inferior education, but also that they were explicitly taught that they were inferior to whites.

Photograph by Peter Magubane

Mandela wrote to his wife, "I find it difficult to believe that I will never see Thembi again."

◄ **DOUBLE TRAGEDY:** Mandela poses for a portrait with his eldest son, Thembekile, called Thembi, in the mid-1950s. Thembi would die in an auto accident in 1969, while Mandela was in prison, and the apartheid government refused to grant Mandela permission to attend the funeral. Mandela's mother, Nosekeni Fanny, had died only a year earlier, and Mandela's prison letters from that time reflected his inner turmoil. "I have lost both Thembi and Ma," he wrote to a friend, "and I must confess that the order that had reigned in my soul has almost vanished."

During the Treason Trial, nearly the entire leadership of the ANC was charged with a nationwide conspiracy to overthrow the government.

▶ **THE THREE-YEAR-LONG TREASON TRIAL** (1958–61, with the first arrests in 1956) was an attempt by the apartheid government to destroy the ANC by legal means. Here, during a break in the trial, Mandela, one of 156 defendants charged with high treason, talks to Peter Nthite, a leader of the ANC Youth League. The defendants included nearly the entire leadership of the ANC. They were charged with a nationwide conspiracy to overthrow the government and replace it with a communist state. In 1958 charges were dropped against sixty-one of the defendants, and in 1961 the remaining ninety-five were found not guilty and discharged. Nevertheless, the apartheid government banned the forty-eight-year-old ANC in 1960, forcing it underground and into exile.

Photograph by Peter Magubane

MANDELA TALKS WITH JOURNALIST AND ANC member Ruth First outside the Pretoria courtroom where the preliminary phase of the Treason Trial was held in 1957 and 1958. In 1982, First, a journalist, sociologist, and activist who was a defendant in the trial, was assassinated by a letter bomb sent to her home in exile in neighboring Mozambique by agents of the apartheid government.

Photographs by Bob Gosani (left) and Eli Weinberg (above)

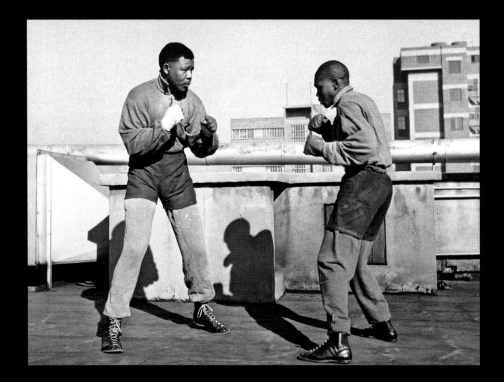

IN AND OUT OF THE RING In 1957, during the run-up to the Treason Trial, Mandela kept fit and relieved the stress that came with being a lawyer, activist, indicted defendant, and father with regular training bouts at boxing champion Jerry Moloi's gym in Soweto.

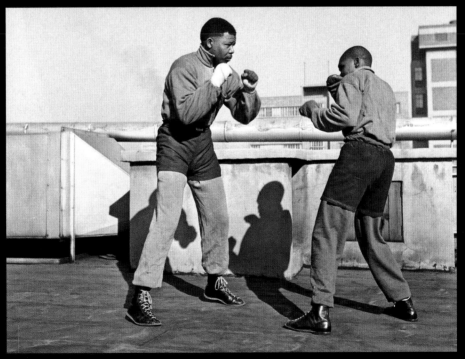

Here he boxes with Moloi for a *Drum* magazine photographer on the roof of a building in downtown Johannesburg. Mandela was intrigued with the body movements and strategies of attack and defeat necessary to pace oneself in boxing. "It was a way of losing myself in something that was not the struggle," he said.

Photographs by Bob Gosani for *Drum* magazine

SOUTH AFRICA'S EVITA: Nelson Rolihlahla Dalibunga Mandela married Nomzamo Winnie Madikizela on June 14, 1958, in a modest ceremony at Bizana in the Eastern Cape. The wedding followed a dramatic courtship and love affair during which Mandela was always either on trial or underground. Nelson and Winnie had two daughters, Zindzi and Zenani.

For most of their married life—Mandela's twenty-seven years in jail—the stunningly charismatic Winnie was the face and voice of the Mandela brand. But following prolonged police harassment and internal banishment in the 1980s, Winnie became an increasingly tragic and eventually disgraced public figure. Nelson and Winnie were separated in 1992, after her conviction for kidnapping a fourteen-year-old anti-apartheid activist who subsequently died from injuries inflicted by her personal gang of young toughs, the so-called Mandela Football Club. They divorced in 1996. Winnie has remained a public figure with a populist following, but has never been far from controversy, and her ambitions to become a leader of the ANC have been thwarted on several occasions.

Photograph (left) by Alf Khumalo

Mandela's stature as a leader and a serious thinker grew throughout the long Treason Trial.

▶ **ANOTHER DAY IN COURT:** During the Treason Trial in October 1958, Mandela leaves the Old Synagogue serving as a court in Pretoria's Church Square with Moses Kotane, secretary general of the South African Communist Party and a prominent ANC leader. The fashionably dressed Mandela's stature as a leader and a serious thinker grew throughout the trial. The years-long Treason Trial placed severe financial pressures on the ANC and largely immobilized its leadership. But Mandela argued that the trial helped sharpen resistance to apartheid and set the scene for a showdown.

Photograph by Jurgen Schadeberg

◄ THE END OF PASSIVE RESISTANCE: Mandela burns his passbook in the wake of the 1960 Sharpeville massacre, when police opened fire on peaceful demonstrators. The demonstrators had planned to offer themselves up for arrest at the local police station rather than carry the hated passbooks that all nonwhite South Africans were required to keep on their persons. Prior to the massacre, Mandela had hoped to ignite a peaceful mass passbook-burning campaign. But when an ANC rival, the more strident Pan Africanist Congress, preemptively staged the ill-fated Sharpeville protest, the window for passive resistance closed. The government clamped down on all protests and banned both the ANC and the PAC, forcing them into exile and turning them toward armed resistance.

▲ ALL SMILES AND LOVE: Mandela is photographed in a classic embrace with his wife, Winnie, in 1962, four years after their wedding. Their smiles were to be short-lived. Following his acquittal in the Treason Trial and the formation of the ANC's military wing, Umkhonto we Sizwe, Mandela went underground for eighteen months and traveled abroad to receive military training and seek financial support for the ANC. When he returned to South Africa, he would be arrested, tried, and sent to prison for the next twenty-seven years.

THE BLACK PIMPERNEL ABROAD: Following his acquittal in the Treason Trial and the formation of the ANC's military wing in 1961, Mandela went underground and traveled abroad to receive military training and raise financial and diplomatic support. During this period Mandela became known as the Black Pimpernel since, like the storybook hero the Scarlet Pimpernel, he was always on the run and ducking detection by government agents. Above, Mandela is seen in London around mid-1962 with his friend Mary Benson from Pretoria. Benson relocated to the UK, where she wrote several books about Mandela and the ANC.

This was Mandela's first visit to what had once been the capital of an empire that covered two-thirds of the globe. Mandela said that as he traveled with his friend and colleague Oliver Tambo in London, he felt ambivalent about its symbols of power: "When I saw the statue of General Jan Smuts [former South African prime minister and founder of the League of Nations] near Westminster Abbey, Oliver and I joked that perhaps someday there would be a statue of us there instead." Mandela recalled this quip when he traveled to London on August 29, 2007, to witness the unveiling of his own statue in the same square.

Photographs by and from Mary Benson

▲ **PARTNERS IN LAW, BROTHERS IN ARMS:** Mandela (right) and Oliver Tambo meet in Addis Ababa, Ethiopia, around mid-1962. Mandela was traveling abroad to win military and diplomatic support for the ANC and its military wing in the struggle to end apartheid. Tambo had gone into exile the previous year, following the Treason Trial. It was now clear that there was no turning back in the confrontation between the ANC and the apartheid regime, and the two leaders had to convince other African states that the ANC had no option but to take up arms against apartheid.

▶ **ALGERIAN MODEL:** When Mandela traveled the world to raise financial support and training for the ANC and its military wing, he visited the headquarters of the Algerian revolutionary army in Morocco near the end of the Algerian civil war. Mandela wrote in *Long Walk to Freedom*, his autobiography, that Algeria was the closest model to the South African liberation struggle "in that the rebels faced a large white settler community that ruled the indigenous majority." Mandela noted the Algerian emphasis on guerrilla warfare as a means of unleashing political and economic forces that could defeat the enemy. Mandela's ANC colleague Robert Resha is second from left.

During his eighteen months on the run, the press dubbed the elusive Mandela the Black Pimpernel.

▶ **DURING THE EIGHTEEN MONTHS** he spent underground in 1961 and 1962, Mandela grew a beard and traveled to the UK, Russia, Algeria, and Ethiopia.

▲ FIRST OF MANY: Winnie Mandela visited her husband many hundreds of times during his twenty-seven years of imprisonment. Winnie stood by him for the entire period, and the two exchanged frequent letters with details of family matters and cryptic political messages to avoid prison censors. Their passionate letters are deeply moving. During this long period of physical separation—she was allowed contact visits only after many years of lobbying—Winnie was the voice of Mandela and the ANC and was widely quoted by foreign news organizations.

▶ XHOSA DRESS: Winnie Mandela attends her husband's trial in Pretoria in the traditional dress of the Xhosa people. It was not the first time that Mandela had been on trial, and it would not be the last.

◄ PALACE OF JUSTICE: Winnie Mandela, wearing a fashionable hat and outfit, attends the opening of the Rivonia Trial at Pretoria's Palace of Justice in December 1963. Behind her, in a black beret, is Nelson Mandela's mother, Nosekeni Fanny. The Rivonia Trial would focus international attention on apartheid and racial injustice in South Africa as never before, and it would take the global anti-apartheid struggle to a new level. The eight defendants, representing the top leadership of the ANC and its military wing, faced charges of high treason and a prosecution that called for the death penalty. The judge handed down eight sentences of life imprisonment, spurring what went on to become a twenty-five-year-long global campaign to end apartheid.

▼ FOLLOWING PAGE: The smile that would charm the whole world a quarter of a century later was already evident in this early 1960s photograph. Mandela was in his early forties and still an impulsive activist with a quick temper.

AN IDEAL FOR WHICH I AM PREPARED TO DIE

April 20, 1964

Nelson Mandela delivered this "statement from the dock" at the opening of the defense case in the Rivonia Trial. At the conclusion of the trial, Mandela, Walter Sisulu, Govan Mbeki, Raymond Mhlaba, Elias Motsoaledi, Andrew Mlangeni, Ahmed Kathrada, and Denis Goldberg were convicted. Mandela was found guilty on four charges of sabotage, and like the others was sentenced to life imprisonment.[1]

I am the First Accused. I hold a bachelor's degree in arts and practiced as an attorney in Johannesburg for a number of years in partnership with Oliver Tambo. I am a convicted prisoner serving five years for leaving the country without a permit and for inciting people to go on strike at the end of May 1961.

At the outset, I want to say that the suggestion made by the state in its opening that the struggle in South Africa is under the influence of foreigners or communists is wholly incorrect. I have done whatever I did, both as an individual and as a leader of my people, because of my experience in South Africa and my own proudly felt African background, and not because of what any outsider might have said.

In my youth, in the Transkei, I listened to the elders of my tribe telling stories of the old days. Amongst the tales they related to me were those of wars fought by our ancestors in defense of the fatherland. The names of Dingane and Bambata, Hintsa and Makana, Squngthi and Dalasile, Moshoeshoe and Sekhukhuni, were praised as the glory of the entire African nation. I hoped then that life might offer

[1] Certain sections of this speech, indicated by ellipses [...], have been omitted. Footnotes have been added to explain certain historical references, and words have been added in brackets [ ] for the same purpose. Spelling and punctuation have been Americanized. This speech, in its entirety, and many others by Mandela, can be found at www.anc.org.za.

me the opportunity to serve my people and make my own humble contribution to their freedom struggle. This is what has motivated me in all that I have done in relation to the charges made against me in this case.

Having said this, I must deal immediately and at some length with the question of violence. Some of the things so far told to the court are true and some are untrue. I do not, however, deny that I planned sabotage. I did not plan it in a spirit of recklessness, nor because I have any love of violence. I planned it as a result of a calm and sober assessment of the political situation that had arisen after many years of tyranny, exploitation, and oppression of my people by the whites.

I admit immediately that I was one of the persons who helped to form Umkhonto we Sizwe[2] and that I played a prominent role in its affairs until I was arrested in August 1962… I, and the others who started the organization, did so for two reasons. Firstly, we believed that as a result of government policy, violence by the African people had become inevitable, and that unless responsible leadership was given to canalize and control the feelings of our people, there would be outbreaks of terrorism which would produce an intensity of bitterness and hostility between the various races of this country which is not produced even by war.

Secondly, we felt that without violence there would be no way open to the African people to succeed in their struggle against the principle of white supremacy. All lawful modes of expressing opposition to this principle had been closed by legislation, and we were placed in a position in which we had either to accept a permanent state of inferiority, or to defy the government. We chose to defy the law. We first broke the law in a way which avoided any recourse to violence. When this form [of defiance] was legislated against, and then the government resorted to a show of force to crush opposition to its policies, only then did we decide to answer violence with violence.

But the violence which we chose to adopt was not terrorism. We who formed Umkhonto were all members of the African National Congress, and had behind us the ANC tradition of nonviolence and negotiation as a means of solving political disputes. We believe that South Africa belongs to all the people who live

---

[2] Spear of the Nation, the military wing of the African National Congress.

in it, and not to one group, be it black or white. We did not want an interracial war, and tried to avoid it to the last minute. If the court is in doubt about this, it will be seen that the whole history of our organization bears out what I have said, and what I will subsequently say, when I describe the tactics which Umkhonto decided to adopt. I want, therefore, to say something about the African National Congress.

The African National Congress was formed in 1912 to defend the rights of the African people which had been seriously curtailed by the South Africa Act, and which were then being threatened by the Native Land Act. For thirty-seven years—that is, until 1949—it adhered strictly to a constitutional struggle. It put forward demands and resolutions; it sent delegations to the government in the belief that African grievances could be settled through peaceful discussion and that Africans could advance gradually to full political rights. But white governments remained unmoved, and the rights of Africans became less instead of becoming greater. In the words of my leader, Chief [Albert] Lutuli, who became president of the ANC in 1952, and who was later awarded the Nobel Peace Prize:

We had to accept a permanent state of inferiority or defy the government. We chose to defy the law.

> Who will deny that thirty years of my life have been spent knocking in vain, patiently, moderately, and modestly, at a closed and barred door? What have been the fruits of moderation? The past thirty years have seen the greatest number of laws restricting our rights and progress, until today we have reached a stage where we have almost no rights at all.

Even after 1949, the ANC remained determined to avoid violence. At this time, however, there was a change from the strictly constitutional means of protest which had been employed in the past. The change was embodied in a decision which

▲ **FREE MANDELA:** Following Mandela's arrest on charges of incitement in August 1962, these women joined Winnie Mandela on the steps of city hall in Johannesburg to demand his immediate release. They also chanted slogans denouncing Dr. Hendrik Verwoerd, the prime minister and perceived architect of apartheid. Verwoerd survived two assassin's bullets, delivered point-blank to the face in 1960, but in 1966, he was stabbed to death by a mixed-race parliamentary messenger while sitting in his seat in Parliament as the bell rang for the start of the day's session.

Photograph by Dennis Lee Royle

was taken to protest against apartheid legislation by peaceful, but unlawful, demonstrations against certain laws. Pursuant to this policy, the ANC launched the Defiance Campaign, in which I was placed in charge of volunteers. This campaign was based on the principles of passive resistance. More than 8,500 people defied apartheid laws and went to jail. Yet there was not a single instance of violence in the course of this campaign on the part of any defier. I, and nineteen [of my] colleagues, were convicted for the role which we played in organizing the campaign, but our sentences were suspended mainly because the judge found that discipline and nonviolence had been stressed throughout. This was the time when the volunteer section of the ANC was established, and when the word Amadelafuka[3] was first used. This was the time when the volunteers were asked to take a pledge to uphold certain principles. Evidence dealing with volunteers and their pledges has been introduced into this case, but completely out of context. The volunteers were not, and are not, the soldiers of a black army pledged to fight a civil war against the whites. They were, and are, dedicated workers who are prepared to lead campaigns initiated by the ANC to distribute leaflets, to organize strikes, or do whatever the particular campaign required. They are called volunteers because they volunteer to face the penalties of imprisonment and whipping which are now prescribed by the legislature for such acts.

During the Defiance Campaign, the Public Safety Act and the Criminal Law Amendment Act were passed. These statutes provided harsher penalties for offenses committed by way of protests against laws. Despite this, the protests continued and the ANC adhered to its policy of nonviolence. In 1956, 156 leading members of the Congress Alliance, including myself, were arrested on a charge of high treason and charged under the Suppression of Communism Act. The nonviolent policy of the ANC was put in issue by the state, but when the court gave judgment some five years later, it found that the ANC did not have a policy of violence. We were acquitted on all counts, which included a count that the ANC sought to set up a communist state in place of the existing regime. The government has always sought to label all its opponents as communists. This allegation has been repeated in the present case, but as I will show, the ANC is not, and never has been, a communist organization.

In 1960 there was the shooting at Sharpeville[4], which resulted in the proclamation of a state of emergency and the declaration of the ANC as an unlawful organization. My colleagues and I, after careful consideration, decided that we would not obey this decree. The African people were not part of the government and did not make the laws by which they were governed. We believed in the words of the Universal Declaration of Human Rights, that "the will of the people shall be the basis of authority of the government," and for us to accept the banning was

[3] "Those who are prepared to make sacrifices."

[4] The Sharpeville massacre, when police fired on an unarmed crowd protesting South Africa's pass laws. The massacre sparked weeks of riots, and is generally considered a turning point in the anti-apartheid movement.

equivalent to accepting the silencing of the Africans for all time. The ANC refused to dissolve, but instead went underground. We believed it was our duty to preserve this organization which had been built up with almost fifty years of unremitting toil. I have no doubt that no self-respecting white political organization would disband itself if declared illegal by a government in which it had no say.

In 1960 the government held a referendum which led to the establishment of the Republic [of South Africa]. Africans, who constituted approximately 70 percent of the population of South Africa, were not entitled to vote, and were not even consulted about the proposed constitutional change. All of us were apprehensive of our future under the proposed white republic, and a resolution was taken to hold an All-In African Conference[5] to call for a national convention, and to organize mass demonstrations on the eve of the unwanted republic, if the government failed to call the convention. The conference was attended by Africans of various political persuasions. I was the secretary of the conference and undertook to be responsible for organizing the national "stay-at-home" which was subsequently called to coincide with the declaration of the republic. As all strikes by Africans are illegal, the person organizing such a strike must avoid arrest. I was chosen to be this person, and consequently I had to leave my home and family and my practice and go into hiding to avoid arrest.

The stay-at-home, in accordance with ANC policy, was to be a peaceful demonstration. Careful instructions were given to organizers and members to avoid any recourse to violence. The government's answer was to introduce new and harsher laws, to mobilize its armed forces, and to send Saracens[6], armed vehicles, and soldiers into the townships in a massive show of force designed to intimidate the people. This was an indication that the government had decided to rule by force alone, and this decision was a milestone on the road to Umkhonto.

Some of this may appear irrelevant to this trial. In fact, I believe none of it is irrelevant because it will, I hope, enable the court to appreciate the attitude eventually adopted by the various persons and bodies concerned in the national

[5] The All-in African Conference, held in Pietermaritzburg, South Africa on March 25-26, 1961, was attended by 1,398 delegates from around the country despite government efforts to hinder it.

[6] Armored troop carriers.

liberation movement… What were we, the leaders of our people, to do? Were we to give in to the show of force and the implied threat against future action, or were we to fight it and, if so, how?

We had no doubt that we had to continue the fight. Anything else would have been abject surrender. Our problem was not whether to fight, but how to continue the fight. We of the ANC had always stood for a nonracial democracy, and we shrank from any action which might drive the races further apart than they already were. But the hard facts were that fifty years of nonviolence had brought the African people nothing but more and more repressive legislation, and fewer and fewer rights. It may not be easy for this court to understand, but it is a fact that for a long time the people had been talking of violence—of the day when they would fight the white man and win back their country—and we, the leaders of the ANC, had

> A government which uses force to maintain its rule teaches the oppressed to use force to oppose it.

nevertheless always prevailed upon them to avoid violence and to pursue peaceful methods. When some of us discussed this in May and June of 1961, it could not be denied that our policy to achieve a nonracial state by nonviolence had achieved nothing, and that our followers were beginning to lose confidence in this policy and were developing disturbing ideas of terrorism.

It must not be forgotten that by this time violence had, in fact, become a feature of the South African political scene. There had been violence in 1957 when the women of Zeerust[7] were ordered to carry passes. There was violence in 1958 with the enforcement of cattle culling in Sekhukhuniland[8]; there was violence in 1959 when the people of Cato Manor[9] protested against pass raids; there was violence in 1960 when the government attempted to impose Bantu Authorities in

[7] A small town approximately 150 miles northwest of Johannesburg.

[8] An area northwest of Johannesburg.

[9] Near Durban, the site of a particularly gruesome attack on police on January 23, 1960.

Pondoland.[10] Thirty-nine Africans died in these disturbances. In 1961 there had been riots in Warmbaths,[11] and all this time the Transkei[12] had been a seething mass of unrest.

Each disturbance pointed clearly to the inevitable growth among Africans of the belief that violence was the only way out. It showed that a government which uses force to maintain its rule teaches the oppressed to use force to oppose it. Already small groups had arisen in the urban areas and were spontaneously making plans for violent forms of political struggle. There now arose a danger that these groups would adopt terrorism against Africans, as well as whites, if not properly directed. Particularly disturbing was the type of violence engendered in places such as Zeerust, Sekhukhuniland, and Pondoland amongst Africans. It was increasingly taking the form, not of struggle against the government—though this is what prompted it—but of civil strife amongst themselves, conducted in such a way that it could not hope to achieve anything other than a loss of life and bitterness.

At the beginning of June 1961, after a long and anxious assessment of the South African situation, I, and some colleagues, came to the conclusion that as violence in this country was inevitable, it would be unrealistic and wrong for African leaders to continue preaching peace and nonviolence at a time when the government met our peaceful demands with force.

This conclusion was not easily arrived at. It was only when all else had failed, when all channels of peaceful protest had been barred to us, that the decision was made to embark on violent forms of political struggle, and to form Umkhonto we Sizwe. We did so not because we desired such a course, but solely because the government had left us with no other choice… I made it clear that if I formed the organization I would at all times subject it to the political guidance of the ANC and would not undertake any different form of activity from that contemplated without the consent of the ANC. And I shall now tell the court how that form of violence came to be determined.

---

[10] A region in the Eastern Cape.

[11] A town north of Pretoria, now known as Bela-Bela.

[12] A region in the Eastern Cape.

As a result of this decision, Umkhonto was formed in November 1961. When we took this decision, and subsequently formulated our plans, the ANC heritage of nonviolence and racial harmony was very much with us. We felt that the country was drifting towards a civil war in which blacks and whites would fight each other. We viewed the situation with alarm. Civil war could mean the destruction of what the ANC stood for. With civil war, racial peace would be more difficult than ever to achieve. We already have examples in South African history of the results of war. It has taken more than fifty years for the scars of the South African War to disappear. How much longer would it take to eradicate the scars of interracial civil war, which could not be fought without a great loss of life on both sides?

▲ **SURE AS THE SUNRISE:** In this 1961 photograph, Mandela displays the sense of purpose and determination that would not only sustain him during twenty-seven years in prison but enable him to tap reserves of character and self-knowledge that turned the tables on his jailers and changed the course of history in his own lifetime.

The avoidance of civil war had dominated our thinking for many years, but when we decided to adopt violence as part of our policy, we realized that we might one day have to face the prospect of such a war. This had to be taken into account in formulating our plans. We required a plan which was flexible and which permitted us to act in accordance with the needs of the times. Above all, the plan had to be one which recognized civil war as the last resort, and left the decision on this question to the future. We did not want to be committed to civil war, but we wanted to be ready if it became inevitable.

Four forms of violence were possible. There is sabotage; there is guerrilla warfare; there is terrorism; and there is open revolution. We chose to adopt the first method and to exhaust it before taking any other decision.

In the light of our political background the choice was a logical one. Sabotage did not involve loss of life, and it offered the best hope for future race relations. Bitterness would be kept to a minimum and, if the policy bore fruit, democratic government could become a reality. This is what we felt at the time, and this is what we said in our manifesto:

> We of Umkhonto we Sizwe have always sought to achieve liberation without bloodshed and civil clash. We hope, even at this late hour, that our first actions will awaken everyone to a realization of the disastrous situation to which the Nationalist policy is leading. We hope that we will bring the government and its supporters to their senses before it is too late, so that both the government and its policies can be changed before matters reach the desperate state of civil war.

The initial plan was based on a careful analysis of the political and economic situation of our country. We believed that South Africa depended to a large extent on foreign capital and foreign trade. We felt that planned destruction of power plants, and interference with rail and telephone communications, would tend to scare away capital from the country, [would] make it more difficult for goods from the industrial areas to reach the seaports on schedule, and would in the long run be a heavy drain on the economic life of the country, thus compelling the voters of the country to reconsider their position.

Attacks on the economic lifelines of the country were to be linked with sabotage on government buildings and other symbols of apartheid. These attacks would serve as a source of inspiration to our people. In addition, they would provide an outlet for those people who were urging the adoption of violent methods and would enable us to give concrete proof to our followers that we had adopted a stronger line and were fighting back against government violence. In addition, if mass action were successfully organized, and mass reprisals taken, we felt that sympathy for our cause would be roused in other countries, and that greater pressure would be brought to bear on the South African government.

This then was the plan. Umkhonto was to perform sabotage, and strict instructions were given to its members right from the start, that on no account were they to injure or kill people in planning or carrying out operations...

[Mandela here discusses the command structure of Umkhonto, which he contended prevented indiscriminate violence.]

Umkhonto had its first operation on 16 December 1961, when government buildings in Johannesburg, Port Elizabeth, and Durban were attacked. The selection of targets is proof of the policy to which I have referred. Had we intended to attack life, we would have selected targets where people congregated and not empty buildings and power stations. The sabotage which was committed before 16 December 1961 was the work of isolated groups and had no connection whatsoever with Umkhonto...

The manifesto of Umkhonto was issued on the day that operations commenced. The response to our actions and manifesto among the white population was characteristically violent. The government threatened to take strong action, and called upon its supporters to stand firm and to ignore the demands of the Africans. The whites failed to respond by suggesting change; they responded to our call by suggesting the *laager*.[13]

[13] A formation used by pioneers in South Africa who would draw wagons into a circle and place cattle and horses on the inside to protect them from raiders or nocturnal animals. In 1800s America, the same approach was used by pioneers who would "circle the wagons" in case of Indian attack.

▲ SHARPEVILLE MASSACRE: On March 21, 1960, apartheid police opened fire on a crowd of approximately seven thousand residents of Sharpeville, a black township south of Johannesburg. The residents were participating in a protest against pass laws organized by the Pan Africanist Congress (PAC), an ANC rival that adopted a more radical Africanist stance in confronting apartheid. The pass laws required Africans to carry identity documents at all times that permitted them to be in the "white" urban areas of South Africa. Sixty-nine people—including eight women and ten children—were killed. The Sharpeville massacre was the spark that led to the creation of the military wings of the ANC and the PAC.

In contrast, the response of the Africans was one of encouragement. Suddenly there was hope again. Things were happening. People in the townships became eager for political news. A great deal of enthusiasm was generated by the initial successes, and people began to speculate on how soon freedom would be obtained.

But we in Umkhonto weighed up the white response with anxiety. The lines were being drawn. The whites and blacks were moving into separate camps, and the prospects of avoiding a civil war were made less. The white newspapers carried reports that sabotage would be punished by death. If this was so, how could we continue to keep Africans away from terrorism?

Already scores of Africans had died as a result of racial friction. In 1920, when the famous leader Masabala[14] was held in Port Elizabeth jail, twenty-four of a group of Africans who had gathered to demand his release were killed by the police and white civilians. In 1921, more than one hundred Africans died in the Bulhoek affair.[15] In 1924, over two hundred Africans were killed when the administrator of South-West Africa led a force against a group which had rebelled against the imposition of [a] dog tax. On 1 May 1950, eighteen Africans died as a result of police shootings during the strike. On 21 March 1960, sixty-nine unarmed Africans died at Sharpeville.

How many more Sharpevilles would there be in the history of our country? And how many more Sharpevilles could the country stand without violence and terror becoming the order of the day? And what would happen to our people when that stage was reached? In the long run we felt certain we must succeed, but at what cost to ourselves and the rest of the country? And if this happened, how could black and white ever live together again in peace and harmony? These were the problems that faced us, and these were our decisions.

Experience convinced us that rebellion would offer the government limitless opportunities for the indiscriminate slaughter of our people. But it was precisely because the soil of South Africa is already drenched with the blood of innocent Africans that we felt it our duty to make preparations as a long-term undertaking to use force in order to defend ourselves against force. If war were inevitable, we wanted the fight to be conducted on terms most favorable to our people. The fight which held out prospects best for us, and the least risk of life to both sides, was guerrilla warfare. We decided, therefore, in our preparations for the future, to make provision for the possibility of guerrilla warfare.

All whites undergo compulsory military training, but no such training was given to Africans. It was in our view essential to build up a nucleus of trained men who would be able to provide the leadership which would be required if guerrilla warfare started. We had to prepare for such a situation before it became too late

[14] Labor leader Samuel Masabala.

[15] On May 24, 1921, 163 people were killed when South African police fired on a charging group of "Israelites," a religious sect that refused to leave a squatters' settlement near Queenstown in the Eastern Cape.

to make proper preparations. It was also necessary to build up a nucleus of men trained in civil administration and other professions, so that Africans would be equipped to participate in the government of this country as soon as they were allowed to do so.

At this stage it was decided that I should attend the Conference of the Pan-African Freedom Movement for Central, East, and Southern Africa, which was to be held early in 1962 in Addis Ababa, and, because of our need for preparation, it was also decided that, after the conference, I would undertake a tour of the African states with a view to obtaining facilities for the training of soldiers, and that I would also solicit scholarships for the higher education of matriculated Africans. Training in both fields would be necessary, even if changes came about by peaceful means. Administrators would be necessary who would be willing and able to administer a non-racial state, and so would men be necessary to control the army and police force of such a state.

It was on this note that I left South Africa to proceed to Addis Ababa as a delegate of the ANC. My tour was a success. Wherever I went, I met sympathy for our cause and promises of help. All Africa was united against the stand of white South Africa, and even in London I was received with great sympathy by political leaders, such as Mr. Gaitskell[16] and Mr. Grimond.[17] In Africa I was promised support by such men as Julius Nyerere, now president of Tanganyika; Mr. Kawawa, then prime minister of Tanganyika; Emperor Haile Selassie of Ethiopia; General Abboud, president of the Sudan; Habib Bourguiba, president of Tunisia; Ben Bella, now president of Algeria; Modibo Keita, president of Mali; Leopold Senghor, president of Senegal; Sekou Toure, president of Guinea; President [William] Tubman of Liberia; and Milton Obote, prime minister of Uganda. It was Ben Bella who invited me to visit Oujda, the headquarters of the Algerian Army of National Liberation…

I started to make a study of the art of war and revolution and, whilst abroad, underwent a course in military training. If there was to be guerrilla warfare, I

[16] Hugh Gaitskell (1906-63), the leader of the British Labour Party from 1955 until his death.

[17] Joseph "Jo" Grimond (1913-93), the leader of the British Liberal Party from 1956 to 1967 and again briefly in 1976.

wanted to be able to stand and fight with my people and to share the hazards of war with them. Notes of lectures which I received in Algeria are contained in Exhibit 16, produced in evidence. Summaries of books on guerrilla warfare and military strategy have also been produced. I have already admitted that these documents are in my writing, and I acknowledge that I made these studies to equip myself for the role which I might have to play if the struggle drifted into guerrilla warfare. I approached this question as every African nationalist should do. I was completely objective. The court will see that I attempted to examine all types of authority on the subject—from the East and from the West—going back to the classic work of Clausewitz,[18] and covering such a variety as Mao Tse-Tung and Che Guevara on the one hand, and the writings on the Anglo-Boer War on the other. Of course, these notes are merely summaries of the books I read and do not contain my personal views.

If there was to be guerrilla warfare, I wanted to be able to stand and fight with my people.

I also made arrangements for our recruits to undergo military training. But here it was impossible to organize any scheme without the co-operation of the ANC offices in Africa. I consequently obtained the permission of the ANC in South Africa to do this. To this extent, then, there was a departure from the original decision of the ANC, but it applied outside South Africa only. The first batch of recruits actually arrived in Tanganyika when I was passing through that country on my way back to South Africa.

I returned to South Africa and reported to my colleagues on the results of my trip. On my return I found that there had been little alteration in the political scene save that the threat of a death penalty for sabotage had now become a fact. The attitude of my colleagues in Umkhonto was much the same as it had been before I left. They were feeling their way cautiously and felt that it would be a long time before the possibilities of sabotage were exhausted. In fact, the

---

[18] Carl von Clausewitz (1780-1831), Prussian soldier, military historian, and military theorist who is most famous for his military treatise *On War.*

view was expressed by some that the training of recruits was premature... After a full discussion, however, it was decided to go ahead with the plans for military training because of the fact that it would take many years to build up a sufficient nucleus of trained soldiers to start a guerrilla campaign, and whatever happened, the training would be of value...

The ideological creed of the ANC is, and always has been, the creed of African nationalism. It is not the concept of African nationalism expressed in the cry "Drive the white man into the sea." The African nationalism for which the ANC stands is the concept of freedom and fulfillment for the African people in their own land. The most important political document ever adopted by the ANC is the Freedom Charter. It is by no means a blueprint for a socialist state. It calls for redistribution, but not nationalization, of land. It provides for nationalization of mines, banks, and monopoly industry, because big monopolies are owned by one race only, and without such nationalization racial domination would be perpetuated despite the spread of political power. It would be a hollow gesture to repeal the Gold Law[19] prohibitions against Africans when all gold mines are owned by European companies. In this respect, the ANC's policy corresponds with the old policy of the present Nationalist Party,[20] which for many years had as part of its program the nationalization of the gold mines which, at that time, were controlled by foreign capital.

Under the Freedom Charter, nationalization would take place in an economy based on private enterprise. The realization of the Freedom Charter would open up fresh fields for a prosperous African population of all classes, including the middle class. The ANC has never at any period of its history advocated a revolutionary change in the economic structure of the country, nor has it, to the best of my recollection, ever condemned capitalist society...

[Mandela here discusses at length the relationship between the ANC and the Communist Party in South Africa and abroad. He says that while the ANC has received the party's

[19] A law preventing any nonwhite person from obtaining a license to dig for precious metals or to own land in areas where precious metals were found.

[20] The governing party of South Africa from June 4, 1948, until May 9, 1994. Disbanded in 2005. Its policies included apartheid and the promotion of white Afrikaner culture.

support and shares some of its views, there are clearly defined differences between commu-nism and the ANC's brand of African nationalism. This is relevant because South Africa's Suppression of Communism Act of 1950 formally banned the Communist Party of South Africa and proscribed the ideology of communism. The act was used to attack the ANC and other anti-apartheid organizations. Most of the act was repealed in 1982 by Internal Security Act No. 74.]

I have always regarded myself, in the first place, as an African patriot. After all, I was born in Umtata, forty-six years ago. My guardian was my cousin, who was the acting paramount chief of Tembuland, and I am related both to the present paramount chief of Tembuland, Sabata Dalindyebo, and to Kaizer Matanzima, the chief minister of the Transkei.

Today I am attracted by the idea of a classless society, an attraction which springs in part from Marxist reading and in part from my admiration of the structure and organization of early African societies in this country. The land, then the main means of production, belonged to the tribe. There were no rich or poor and there was no exploitation.

It is true, as I have already stated, that I have been influenced by Marxist thought. But this is also true of many of the leaders of the new independent states. Such widely different persons as Gandhi, Nehru, Nkrumah,[21] and Nasser[22] all ac-knowledge this fact. We all accept the need for some form of socialism to enable our people to catch up with the advanced countries of this world and to overcome their legacy of extreme poverty. But this does not mean we are Marxists.

Indeed, for my own part, I believe that it is open to debate whether the Com-munist Party has any specific role to play at this particular stage of our political struggle. The basic task at the present moment is the removal of race discrimina-tion and the attainment of democratic rights on the basis of the Freedom Charter. Insofar as that party furthers this task, I welcome its assistance. I realize that it is one of the means by which people of all races can be drawn into our struggle.

[21] Kwame Nkrumah (1909-72), the leader of Ghana from 1952 to 1966.

[22] Gamal Abdel Nasser (1918-70), the president of Egypt from 1956 until his death.

From my reading of Marxist literature and from conversations with Marxists, I have gained the impression that communists regard the parliamentary system of the West as undemocratic and reactionary. But, on the contrary, I am an admirer of such a system. The Magna Carta, the Petition of Rights, and the Bill of Rights are documents which are held in veneration by democrats throughout the world.

I have great respect for British political institutions and for the country's system of justice. I regard the British parliament as the most democratic institution in the world, and the independence and impartiality of its judiciary never fail to arouse my admiration. The American Congress, that country's doctrine of separation of powers, as well as the independence of its judiciary, arouses in me similar sentiments.

I have been influenced in my thinking by both West and East. All this has led me to feel that in my search for a political formula, I should be absolutely impartial and objective. I should tie myself to no particular system of society other than [that] of socialism. I must leave myself free to borrow the best from the West and from the East…

[Mandela here discusses foreign and communist-bloc financing of Umkhonto activities.]

Our fight is against real, and not imaginary, hardships or, to use the language of the state prosecutor, "so-called hardships." Basically, we fight against two features which are the hallmarks of African life in South Africa and which are entrenched by legislation which we seek to have repealed. These features are poverty and lack of human dignity, and we do not need communists or so-called "agitators" to teach us about these things.

South Africa is the richest country in Africa, and could be one of the richest countries in the world. But it is a land of extremes and remarkable contrasts. The whites enjoy what may well be the highest standard of living in the world, whilst Africans live in poverty and misery. Forty percent of the Africans live in hopelessly overcrowded and, in some cases, drought-stricken reserves, where soil erosion and the overworking of the soil makes it impossible for them to live properly off the land. Thirty percent are laborers, labor tenants, and squatters on white farms and work and live under conditions similar to those of the serfs of the Middle Ages. The other 30 percent live in towns where they have developed economic and social habits which bring them closer in many respects to white standards. Yet most Africans, even in this group, are impoverished by low incomes and high cost of living.

The highest-paid and the most prosperous section of urban African life is in Johannesburg. Yet their actual position is desperate. The latest figures were given on 25 March 1964 by Mr. Carr, manager of the Johannesburg Non-European Affairs Department. The poverty datum line for the average African family in Johannesburg, according to Mr. Carr's department, is R42.84 per month. He showed that the average monthly wage is R32.24 and that 46 percent of all African families in Johannesburg do not earn enough to keep them going.

Poverty goes hand in hand with malnutrition and disease. The incidence of malnutrition and deficiency diseases is very high amongst Africans. Tuberculosis, pellagra, kwashiorkor, gastroenteritis, and scurvy bring death and destruction of health. The incidence of infant mortality is one of the highest in the world. According to the medical officer of health for Pretoria, tuberculosis kills forty people a day, almost all Africans, and in 1961 there were 58,491 new cases reported. These diseases not only destroy the vital organs of the body, but they result in retarded mental conditions and lack of initiative, and reduce powers of concentration. The secondary results of such conditions affect the whole community and the standard of work performed by African laborers.

The complaint of Africans, however, is not only that they are poor and the whites are rich, but that the laws which are made by the whites are designed to preserve this situation. There are two ways to break out of poverty. The first is by formal education, and the second is by the worker acquiring a greater skill at his work and thus higher wages. As far as Africans are concerned, both these avenues of advancement are deliberately curtailed by legislation.

The present government has always sought to hamper Africans in their search for education. One of their early acts, after coming into power, was to stop subsidies for African school feeding. Many African children who attended schools depended on this supplement to their diet. This was a cruel act.

There is compulsory education for all white children at virtually no cost to their parents, be they rich or poor. Similar facilities are not provided for the African children, though there are some who receive such assistance. African children, however, generally have to pay more for their schooling than whites.

According to figures quoted by the South African Institute of Race Relations in its 1963 journal, approximately 40 percent of African children in the age group between seven [and] fourteen do not attend school. For those who do attend school, the standards are vastly different from those afforded to white children. In 1960–61 the per capita government spending on African students at state-aided schools was estimated at R12.46. In the same years, the per capita spending on white children in the Cape Province (which are the only figures available to me) was R144.57. Although there are no figures available to me, it can be stated, without doubt, that the white children on whom R144.57 per head was being spent all came from wealthier homes than African children on whom R12.46 per head was being spent.

The present prime minister said, "Natives will be taught from childhood to realize that equality with Europeans is not for them."

The quality of education is also different. According to the Bantu Educational Journal, only 5,660 African children in the whole of South Africa passed their Junior Certificate in 1962, and in that year only 362 passed matric[ulation].[23] This is presumably consistent with the policy of Bantu education about which the present prime minister said, during the debate on the Bantu Education Bill in 1953:

When I have control of Native education I will reform it so that Natives will be taught from childhood to realize that equality with Europeans is

[23] The Junior Certificate examination was generally taken by white children at the age of fifteen, and they could not normally leave school before this. "Matriculation" was taken two years later and qualified students for higher education. Without matriculation, they could not attend university.

not for them… People who believe in equality are not desirable teachers for Natives. When my department controls Native education it will know for what class of higher education a Native is fitted, and whether he will have a chance in life to use his knowledge.

The other main obstacle to the economic advancement of the African is the industrial color-bar under which all the better jobs of industry are reserved for whites only. Moreover, Africans who do obtain employment in the unskilled and semiskilled occupations which are open to them are not allowed to form trade unions which have recognition under the Industrial Conciliation Act. This means that strikes of African workers are illegal, and that they are denied the right of collective bargaining which is permitted to the better-paid white workers. The discrimination in the policy of successive South African governments towards African workers is demonstrated by the so-called "civilized labor policy" under which sheltered, unskilled government jobs are found for those white workers who cannot make the grade in industry, at wages which far exceed the earnings of the average African employee in industry.

The government often answers its critics by saying that Africans in South Africa are economically better off than the inhabitants of the other countries in Africa. I do not know whether this statement is true and doubt whether any comparison can be made without regard to the cost-of-living index in such countries. But even if it is true, as far as the African people are concerned it is irrelevant. Our complaint is not that we are poor by comparison with people in other countries, but that we are poor by comparison with the white people in our own country, and that we are prevented by legislation from altering this imbalance.

The lack of human dignity experienced by Africans is the direct result of the policy of white supremacy. White supremacy implies black inferiority. Legislation designed to preserve white supremacy entrenches this notion. Menial tasks in South Africa are invariably performed by Africans. When anything has to be carried or cleaned, the white man will look around for an African to do it for him, whether the African is employed by him or not. Because of this sort of attitude, whites tend to regard Africans as a separate breed. They do not look upon them as people with families of their own. They do not realize that they have emotions; that they fall in love like white people do; that they want to be with their wives and children like white people want to be with theirs; that they want to earn enough money to support their families properly, to feed and clothe them and send them to school. And what "house-boy" or "garden-boy" or laborer can ever hope to do this?

> I have fought against white domination and I have fought against black domination.

Pass laws, which to the Africans are among the most hated bits of legislation in South Africa, render any African liable to police surveillance at any time. I doubt whether there is a single African male in South Africa who has not at some stage had a brush with the police over his pass. Hundreds and thousands of Africans are thrown into jail each year under pass laws. Even worse than this is the fact that pass laws keep husband and wife apart and lead to the breakdown of family life.

Poverty and the breakdown of family life have secondary effects. Children wander about the streets of the townships because they have no schools to go to, or no money to enable them to go to school, or no parents at home to see that they go to school, because both parents, if there be two, have to work to keep the family alive. This leads to a breakdown in moral standards, to an alarming rise in illegitimacy, and to growing violence which erupts not only politically but everywhere. Life in the townships is dangerous. There is not a day that goes by without somebody being stabbed or assaulted. And violence is carried out of the townships in the white living areas. People are afraid to walk alone in the streets after dark. Housebreakings and robberies are increasing, despite the fact that the death sentence can now be imposed for such offenses. Death sentences cannot cure the festering sore.

Africans want to be paid a living wage. Africans want to perform work which they are capable of doing, and not work which the government declares them to be capable of. Africans want to be allowed to live where they obtain work, and not be endorsed out of an area because they were not born there. Africans want to be allowed to own land in places where they work, and not to be obliged to live in rented houses which they can never call their own. Africans want to be part of the general population, and not confined to living in their own ghettoes. African men want to have their wives and children to live with them where they work, and not be forced into an unnatural existence in men's hostels. African women want to be with their menfolk and not be left permanently widowed in the reserves. Africans want to be allowed out after eleven o'clock at night and not to be confined to their rooms like little children. Africans want to be allowed to travel in their own country and to seek work where they want to, and not where the Labor Bureau tells them to. Africans want a just share in the whole of South Africa; they want security and a stake in society.

Above all, we want equal political rights, because without them our disabilities will be permanent. I know this sounds revolutionary to the whites in this country, because the majority of voters will be Africans. This makes the white man fear democracy.

But this fear cannot be allowed to stand in the way of the only solution which will guarantee racial harmony and freedom for all. It is not true that the enfranchisement of all will result in racial domination. Political division, based on color, is entirely artificial, and when it disappears, so will the domination of one color group by another. The ANC has spent half a century fighting against racialism. When it triumphs, it will not change that policy.

This, then, is what the ANC is fighting. Their struggle is a truly national one. It is a struggle of the African people, inspired by their own suffering and their own experience. It is a struggle for the right to live.

During my lifetime I have dedicated myself to this struggle of the African people. I have fought against white domination and I have fought against black domination. I have cherished the ideal of a democratic and free society in which all persons live together in harmony and with equal opportunities. It is an ideal which I hope to live for and to achieve. But if needs be, it is an ideal for which I am prepared to die.

Mandela wrote in his autobiography, "Prison not only robs you of your freedom, it attempts to take away your identity."

▶ **MANDELA AND SISULU:** Nelson Mandela and Walter Sisulu talk in the prison courtyard on Robben Island in 1964. It was the only occasion when Mandela consented to be photographed in prison, and then only on the condition that Sisulu join him. Sisulu, who died in 2003, two weeks before his ninety-first birthday, was six years older than Mandela. He recruited Mandela into the ANC and served as Mandela's mentor throughout their twenty-seven years together in prison and during Mandela's first four years of freedom, when Sisulu served as ANC deputy president. Mandela said Sisulu's death left a void in his life. In an interview after he stepped down as president, Mandela said that Sisulu was "almost like a saint" when it came to taking care of the needs of others. "I learned a great deal from him. He led from behind and put others in front. But he reversed the position in times of danger. Then he chose to be in the front line."

Photograph as printed in the *Daily Telegraph*, London

IN 1964, THE APARTHEID GOVERNMENT invited the *Daily Telegraph*, a conservative British newspaper, to send a reporter and a photographer to Robben Island prison to show the outside world that the Rivonia trialists were being held in humane conditions. In the photograph on the left, prisoners in the first row are breaking stones into gravel suitable for paving roads on the island, while prisoners in the second row are repairing torn mailbags. The above photo is a close-up of Mandela sewing a mailbag. The prisoners were well aware that they were being used for government propaganda purposes. In 1977, when authorities brought a larger group of South African journalists and a television team to the island for the same purpose, Mandela and twenty-eight other prisoners sent a strongly worded protest letter to prison authorities.

UNITE! MOBILIZE! FIGHT ON!

Between the Anvil of United Mass Action and the Hammer of the Armed Struggle, We Shall Crush Apartheid!

This message from Nelson Mandela was written in response to the Soweto uprising of 1976 and published by the African National Congress on June 10, 1980, with an introduction by Oliver "O.R." Tambo, who was president of the African National Congress from 1967 until 1991 and co-founder, with Nelson Mandela and Walter Sisulu, of the ANC Youth League.[1]

The African National Congress brings you this urgent call to unity and mass action by political prisoners on Robben Island to all patriots of our motherland. Nelson Mandela and hundreds of our comrades have been in the racist regime's prisons for more than seventeen years. This message by Nelson Mandela addressed to the struggling masses of our country was written to deal with the present crisis gripping our enemy and in the aftermath of the Soweto uprisings [of 1976]. It was smuggled out of Robben Island prison under very

◄ **ON JUNE 16, 1976, THE STUDENTS OF SOWETO,** impatient with the acquiescence of their parents' generation, took to the streets and confronted the firepower of the apartheid government. They protested the imposition of Afrikaans (the Dutch-based language of white settlers) as the language of instruction in schools. Hundreds of students were killed in the confrontations that ensued, and thousands were injured. The uprising marked a sudden radicalization of the anti-apartheid struggle and gave encouragement to ANC prisoners serving time on Robben Island. Mandela wrote that the young newcomers sent to Robben Island during the Soweto uprising turned the prison upside down. "They were brave, hostile, and aggressive. They would not take orders and shouted *amandla* (power) at every opportunity."

difficult conditions and has taken over two years to reach us. Nonetheless, we believe the message remains fresh and valid and should be presented to our people. [Mandela's] call to unity and mass action is of particular importance in this Year of the Charter—[the] twenty-fifth anniversary of the Freedom Charter.[2] The ANC urges you to respond to this call and make 1980 a year of united mass struggle.

RACISTS RULE BY THE GUN! The gun has played an important part in our history. The resistance of the black man to white colonial intrusion was crushed by the gun. Our struggle to liberate ourselves from white domination is held in check by force of arms. From conquest to the present, the story is the same. Successive white regimes have repeatedly massacred unarmed defenseless blacks. And wherever and whenever they have pulled out their guns, the ferocity of their fire has been trained on the African people.

Apartheid is the embodiment of the racialism, repression, and inhumanity of all previous white supremacist regimes. To see the real face of apartheid we must look beneath the veil of constitutional formulas, deceptive phrases, and playing with words.

The rattle of gunfire and the rumbling of Hippo armored vehicles since June 1976 have once again torn aside that veil. Spread across the face of our country, in black townships, the racist army and police have been pouring a hail of bullets, killing and maiming hundreds of black men, women, and children. The toll of the dead and injured already surpasses that of all past massacres carried out by this regime.

[1] This message is reproduced in its entirety. Footnotes have been added to explain certain historical references, and words have been added in brackets [ ] for the same purpose. Spelling and punctuation have been Americanized. This speech, and many others by Mandela, can be found at www.anc.org.za.

[2] The statement of core principles of The South African Congress Alliance, which included The African National Congress, The South African Indian Congress, The South African Congress of Democrats and The Coloured People's Congress. The Freedom Charter was adopted at the Congress of the People, in Kliptown, South Africa on June 26, 1955. It states, inter alia, "The people shall govern... All national groups shall have equal rights... The people shall share the country's wealth... All shall be equal before the law."

Apartheid is the rule of the gun and the hangman. The Hippo, the FN rifle, and the gallows are its true symbols. These remain the easiest resort, the ever-ready solution of the race-mad rulers of South Africa.

VAGUE PROMISES, GREATER REPRESSION... In the midst of the present crisis, while our people count the dead and nurse the injured, they ask themselves: what lies ahead? From our rulers we can expect nothing. They are the ones who give orders to the soldier crouching over his rifle. Theirs is the spirit that moves the finger that caresses the trigger.

Vague promises, tinkerings with the machinery of apartheid, constitution juggling, massive arrests and detentions side by side with renewed overtures aimed at weakening and forestalling the unity of us blacks and dividing the forces of change—these are the fixed paths along which they will move. For they are neither capable nor willing to heed the verdict of the masses, of our people.

THE VERDICT OF JUNE 16! [3] That verdict is loud and clear: apartheid has failed. Our people remain unequivocal in its rejection. The young and the old, parent and child, all reject it. At the forefront of this 1976–77 wave of unrest were our students and youth. They come from the universities, high schools and even primary schools. They are a generation whose whole education has been under the diabolical design of the racists to poison the minds and brainwash our children into docile subjects of apartheid rule. But after more than twenty years of Bantu education, the circle is closed and nothing demonstrates the utter bankruptcy of apartheid as the revolt of our youth.

---

[3] On June 16, 1976, high school students in the black Johannesburg township of Soweto began protesting for better education—specifically, they did not want to be taught in the Afrikaans language of the white Dutch settlers, which Desmond Tutu called "the language of the oppressor." South African police responded with tear gas and live bullets. An estimated 200 to 600 people died, many of them students. June 16 is commemorated today by a South African national holiday, Youth Day, which honors all the young people who lost their lives in the struggle against apartheid and Bantu education.

The evils, the cruelty, and the inhumanity of apartheid have been there from its inception. And all blacks—Africans, Coloreds,[4] and Indians—have opposed it all along the line. What is now unmistakable, what the current wave of unrest has sharply highlighted, is this: that despite all the window-dressing and smooth talk, apartheid has become intolerable.

This awareness reaches over and beyond the particulars of our enslavement. The measure of this truth is the recognition by our people that under apartheid our lives, individually and collectively, count for nothing.

UNITE! We face an enemy that is deep-rooted, an enemy entrenched and determined not to yield. Our march to freedom is long and difficult. But both within and beyond our borders, the prospects of victory grow bright.

The first condition for victory is black unity. Every effort to divide the blacks—to woo and pit one black group against another—must be vigorously repulsed. Our people—African, Colored, Indian, and democratic whites—must be united into a single massive and solid wall of resistance, of united mass action.

Our struggle is growing sharper. This is not the time for the luxury of division and disunity. At all levels and in every walk of life we must close ranks. Within the ranks of the people, differences must be submerged to the achievement of a single goal—the complete overthrow of apartheid and racist domination.

VICTORY IS CERTAIN! The revulsion of the world against apartheid is growing, and the frontiers of white supremacy are shrinking. Mozambique and Angola are free, and the war of liberation gathers force in Namibia and Zimbabwe. The soil of our country is destined to be the scene of the fiercest fight and the sharpest battles to rid our continent of the last vestiges of white minority rule.

---

[4] An ethnic group of mixed-race people who possess some sub-Saharan African ancestry, but not enough to be considered black under the apartheid laws of South Africa. They often possess substantial ancestry from Europe, Indonesia, India, Madagascar, Malaya, Mozambique, Mauritius, St. Helena, or southern Africa.

The world is on our side. The OAU,[5] the UN, and the anti-apartheid movement continue to put pressure on the racist rulers of our country. Every effort to isolate South Africa adds strength to our struggle.

At all levels of our struggle, within and outside the country, much has been achieved and much remains to be done. But victory is certain!

WE SALUTE ALL OF YOU! We who are confined within the grey walls of the Pretoria regime's prisons reach out to our people. With you we count those who have perished by means of the gun and the hangman's rope. We salute all of you—the living, the injured, and the dead. For you have dared to rise up against the tyrant's might.

Even as we bow at their graves we remember this: the dead live on as martyrs in our hearts and minds, a reproach to our disunity and the host of shortcomings that accompany divisions among the oppressed, a spur to our efforts to close ranks, and a reminder that the freedom of our people is yet to be won.

We face the future with confidence. For the guns that serve apartheid cannot render it unconquerable. Those who live by the gun shall perish by the gun.

UNITE! MOBILIZE! FIGHT ON! Between the anvil of united mass action and the hammer of the armed struggle we shall crush apartheid and white minority racist rule.

AMANDLA NGAWETHU! [6] *MATLA KE A RONA!* [7]

---

[5] The Organization of African Unity (1963–2002), an international organization of African states; later replaced by the African Union.

[6] Roughly, "Power to the People" or "Power is Ours" in the Nguni languages of southern Africa, which include isiXhosa, isiZulu, isiSwazi and isiN'dbele. Often used in call and response.

[7] The same phrase in the Sesotho languange.

◄ WINNIE'S OWN DEFIANCE CAMPAIGN: Winnie Mandela was under constant surveillance by apartheid security police during her husband's twenty-seven-year incarceration. She became the voice of the Mandelas and the face of the anti-apartheid struggle abroad. Even when she was banished for eight years to the remote rural town of Brandfort (1977–85), she continued to be interviewed by foreign news organizations. When her Brandfort house was firebombed in 1985, she defied her banning order and returned to Johannesburg. There she began to indulge in conduct that caused growing concern among the exiled ANC leaders. Here she is seen in Soweto township, outside Johannesburg, shortly after she defied her banning order.

Photograph by Louise Gubb

▼ FOLLOWING PAGES: Over time, the Free Mandela movement gathered strength worldwide. In June 1988, a tribute concert was held to commemorate Nelson Mandela's seventieth birthday at a packed Wembley Stadium. The origins of the concert dated back to 1986, with the formation in Britain of Artists Against Apartheid. The organizers, Jerry Dammers and Dali Tambo, invited a host of musicians to take part in a Freedom Festival on Clapham Common in London. An estimated 100,000 people joined the march to the common before the concert, and at the height of the afternoon, an estimated 250,000 gathered to listen to the artists and to representatives of the ANC, SWAPO (the South West Africa People's Organization), and the British Anti-Apartheid Movement.

Photograph by Gideon Mendel

▶ **THE NELSON MANDELA 70TH BIRTHDAY** tribute concert, held at London's Wembly Stadium in June 1988, was broadcast live to more than 600 million people in sixty-seven countries. It was hailed as the biggest pop-political event of all time and dramatically raised the international profile and respectability of the ANC, increasing pressure on the apartheid government to release Mandela. The concert drew top performers and transformed the careers of emerging stars such as Tracy Chapman. In April 1990, a second concert packed Wembley to celebrate Mandela's freedom.

Photograph by Ebet Roberts

▼ **FOLLOWING PAGES:** Robben Island, set in Table Bay with Table Mountain and Devil's Peak in the background, has been used by its Dutch, British, and Afrikaner rulers as a place to isolate, banish, and imprison people since Jan van Riebeeck of the Dutch East India Company landed there in 1652 and created a supply station. Situated about four miles (seven kilometers) from Cape Town in the cold, often rough Atlantic Ocean, Robben Island—which is named after the Dutch word for seal (*robbe*)—has also served as a leper colony and an animal quarantine station, and was part of South Africa's defenses on the side of the Allied forces during World War II. Mandela, who spent nineteen years on the island (1963–82) before being transferred to a mainland prison in Cape Town for eight years, is the island's most famous prisoner. But those who have died and been imprisoned on the island include a famous Muslim cleric, Sayed Abdurahman Moturu (1740s–54), two African chiefs who resisted colonialism, and two Xhosa prophets who clashed with the British. Many of the founding leaders of democratic South Africa served time on the island for convictions relating to their anti-apartheid activities. Robben Island was declared a World Heritage Site in December 1999, shortly after Mandela stepped down as the country's first black president.

Photograph by Louise Gubb

▶ BEGINNING ANEW: "As I finally walked through those gates I felt—even at the age of seventy-one—that my life was beginning anew," Mandela recalls in his autobiography, *Long Walk to Freedom.* "When I was among the crowd I raised my right fist, and there was a roar. I had not been able to do that for twenty-seven years and it gave me a surge of strength and joy." It was a moment in history when myth and reality merged and time seemed to stand still. Mandela, who had to wait an hour past the appointed time for his release to allow key colleagues time to arrive, was clearly bewildered and even alarmed by the size of the crowd and the frenzy of jostling journalists. He soon recovered his composure and prepared for the drive to Cape Town's Grand Parade, where he gave his first public speech after twenty-seven years in jail. He had worked on the speech with key leaders of the anti-apartheid movement that morning and was already finding out that life outside prison would be an endless series of compromises. He didn't get to make his first speech where he wanted, and he didn't get to spend his first night of freedom where he had suggested. But he could not have hoped for a more hospitable refuge than the home of the archbishop of Cape Town, Archbishop Desmond Tutu, where he spent that first night.

◀ THE MULTITUDE: After his release from prison, a vast multiracial crowd awaited Mandela's arrival at Cape Town's Grand Parade, a public meeting area at the heart of the city that adjoins city hall, where Mandela was due to deliver his first public speech in twenty-seven years. The automobile in which Mandela was traveling was mobbed by the overexcited crowd, which had spent hours waiting in the midsummer heat. "Then people began to jump on the car in their excitement... others began to shake it and at that moment I began to worry. I felt that crowd might very well kill us with their love," Mandela wrote in his autobiography.

Mandela did not make the conciliatory speech that commentators and dignitaries had hoped for. He recommitted himself to the struggle to end apartheid as a loyal and obedient servant of the ANC, by whatever means necessary, including armed struggle and international sanctions. But he did describe South Africa's leader, F. W. de Klerk, who had ordered his release, as a "man of integrity"—a description that soon became the source of considerable controversy.

Photograph by Louise Gubb

UPON RELEASE FROM PRISON

Cape Town, South Africa, February 11, 1990

Friends, comrades, and fellow South Africans: I greet you all in the name of peace, democracy, and freedom for all.[1]

I stand here before you not as a prophet but as a humble servant of you, the people. Your tireless and heroic sacrifices have made it possible for me to be here today. I therefore place the remaining years of my life in your hands.

On this day of my release, I extend my sincere and warmest gratitude to the millions of my compatriots and those in every corner of the globe who have campaigned tirelessly for my release. I send special greetings to the people of Cape Town, this city, which has been my home for three decades. Your mass marches and other forms of struggle have served as a constant source of strength to all political prisoners.

I salute the African National Congress. It has fulfilled our every expectation in its role as leader of the great march to freedom. I salute our [ANC] president, Comrade Oliver Tambo, for leading the ANC even under the most difficult circumstances. I salute the rank-and-file members of the ANC. You have sacrificed life and limb in the pursuit of the noble cause of our struggle. I salute combatants of Umkhonto we Sizwe[2] like Solomon Mahlangu[3] and

---

[1] This speech is reproduced in its entirety. Footnotes have been added to explain certain historical references, and words have been added in brackets [ ] for the same purpose. Spelling and punctuation have been Americanized. This speech, and many others by Mandela, can be found at www.anc.org.za.

[2] Spear of the Nation, the military wing of the African National Congress.

[3] A leader of Umkhonto we Sizwe, executed by the apartheid regime on April 6, 1989.

Ashley Kriel,[4] who have paid the ultimate price for the freedom of all South Africans.

I salute the South African Communist Party for its sterling contribution to the struggle for democracy. You have survived forty years of unrelenting persecution. The memory of great communists like Moses Kotane, Yusuf Dadoo, Bram Fischer, and Moses Mabhida[5] will be cherished for generations to come. I salute General Secretary [of the

[4] A "Coloured" activist shot by police in 1987.

[5] All anti-apartheid activists. Fischer, born a pedigreed member of the Afrikaner establishment, was a lawyer for the defense in the Treason Trial (1956–61) and was Mandela's lead lawyer at the Rivonia Trial (1963–64), where Mandela was sentenced to life in prison. Fischer himself was sentenced to life imprisonment in 1966 under the Suppression of Communism Act. He died in 1975.

▲ **IN WHAT WAS TO BECOME** a familiar if incongruous sight, the seventy-one-year-old Mandela, dressed in his finest suit and with his necktie arranged in a perfect Windsor knot, acknowledges the massive crowd at his first public rally in Soweto with a clenched-fist black power salute. With the carriage of a member of the British aristocracy and the bearing of a royal Thembu chief, Mandela would present himself as a "humble servant of you the people" and recommit himself to the freedom struggle of the ANC.

Photograph by Peter Turnley

South African Communist Party] Joe Slovo, one of our finest patriots. We are heartened by the fact that the alliance between ourselves and the [Communist] Party remains as strong as it always was.

I salute the United Democratic Front, the National Education Crisis Committee, the South African Youth Congress, the Transvaal and Natal Indian Congresses and COSATU,[6] and the many other formations of the mass democratic movement.

I also salute the Black Sash[7] and the National Union of South African Students. We note with pride that you have acted as the conscience of white South Africa. Even during the darkest days in the history of our struggle, you held the flag of liberty high. The large-scale mass mobilization of the past few years is one of the key factors which led to the opening of the final chapter of our struggle.

I extend my greetings to the working class of our country. Your organized strength is the pride of our movement. You remain the most dependable force in the struggle to end exploitation and oppression. I pay tribute to the many religious communities who carried the campaign for justice forward when the organizations for our people were silenced. I greet the traditional leaders of our country. Many of you continue to walk in the footsteps of great heroes like Hintsa[8] and Sekhukhune.[9]

I pay tribute to the endless heroism of youth, you, the young lions. You, the young lions, have energized our entire struggle. I pay tribute to the mothers and wives and sisters of our nation. You are the rock-hard foundation of our struggle. Apartheid has inflicted more pain on you than on anyone else.

On this occasion, we thank the world community for their great contribution to the anti-apartheid struggle. Without your support our struggle would not have reached this advanced stage. The sacrifice of the frontline states will be remembered by South Africans forever.

[6] The Congress of South African Trade Unions.

[7] A nonviolent white women's anti-apartheid organization founded in 1955.

[8] Hintsa ka Khawuta (1789–1835), also known as Hintsa the Great, a Xhosa chieftain barbarously killed by British soldiers.

[9] Sekhukhune (1814–82), king of the Marota people of what is now northern South Africa. He resisted the Boers and the British.

My salutations would be incomplete without expressing my deep appreciation for the strength given to me during my long and lonely years in prison by my beloved wife and family. I am convinced that your pain and suffering was far greater than my own.

Before I go any further, I wish to make the point that I intend making only a few preliminary comments at this stage. I will make a more complete statement only after I have had the opportunity to consult with my comrades.

Today the majority of South Africans, black and white, recognize that apartheid has no future. It has to be ended by our own decisive mass action in order to build peace and security. The mass campaign of defiance and other actions of our organization and people can only culminate in the establishment of democracy. The destruction caused by apartheid on our subcontinent is incalculable. The fabric of family life of millions of my people has been shattered. Millions are homeless and unemployed. Our economy lies in ruins and our people are embroiled in political strife. Our resort to the armed struggle in 1960 with the formation of the military wing of the ANC, Umkhonto we Sizwe, was a purely defensive action against the violence of apartheid. The factors which necessitated the armed struggle still exist today. We have no option but to continue. We express the hope that a climate conducive to a negotiated settlement will be created soon so that there may no longer be the need for the armed struggle.

I am a loyal and disciplined member of the African National Congress. I am therefore in full agreement with all of its objectives, strategies, and tactics.

The need to unite the people of our country is as important a task now as it always has been. No individual leader is able to take on this enormous task on his own. It is our task as leaders to place our views before our organization and to allow the democratic structures to decide. On the question of democratic practice, I feel duty bound to make the point that a leader of the movement is a person who has been democratically elected at a national conference. This is a principle which must be upheld without any exceptions.

We can no longer wait. Now is the time to intensify the struggle on all fronts.

Today, I wish to report to you that my talks with the government have been aimed at normalizing the political situation in the country. We have not as yet begun discussing the basic demands of the struggle. I wish to stress that I myself have at no time entered into negotiations about the future of our country except to insist on a meeting between the ANC and the government.

Mr. de Klerk[10] has gone further than any other Nationalist president in taking real steps to normalize the situation. However, there are further steps as outlined in the Harare Declaration[11] that have to be met before negotiations on the basic demands of our people can begin. I reiterate our call for, inter alia, the immediate ending of the state of emergency and the freeing of all, and not only some, political prisoners. Only such a normalized situation, which allows for free political activity, can allow us to consult our people in order to obtain a mandate.

The people need to be consulted on who will negotiate and on the content of such negotiations. Negotiations cannot take place above the heads or behind the backs of our people. It is our belief that the future of our country can only be determined by a body which is democratically elected on a nonracial basis. Negotiations on the dismantling of apartheid will have to address the overwhelming demand of our people for a democratic, nonracial, and unitary South Africa. There must be an end to white monopoly on political power

[10] F. W. de Klerk (1936–), the last president of apartheid-era South Africa (1989 to 1994) and leader of the National Party (1989 to 1997).

[11] The 1991 Declaration of the British Commonwealth of Nations that, inter alia, opposed apartheid.

and a fundamental restructuring of our political and economic systems to ensure that the inequalities of apartheid are addressed and our society thoroughly democratized.

It must be added that Mr. de Klerk himself is a man of integrity[12] who is acutely aware of the dangers of a public figure not honoring his undertakings. But as an organization we base our policy and strategy on the harsh reality we are faced with. And this reality is that we are still suffering under the policy of the Nationalist government.

Our struggle has reached a decisive moment. We call on our people to seize this moment so that the process towards democracy is rapid and uninterrupted. We have waited too long for our freedom. We can no longer wait. Now is the time to intensify the struggle on all fronts. To relax our efforts now would be a mistake which generations to come will not be able to forgive. The sight of freedom looming on the horizon should encourage us to redouble our efforts.

It is only through disciplined mass action that our victory can be assured. We call on our white compatriots to join us in the shaping of a new South Africa. The freedom movement is a political home for you too. We call on the international community to continue the campaign to isolate the apartheid regime. To lift sanctions now would be to run the risk of aborting the process towards the complete eradication of apartheid.

Our march to freedom is irreversible. We must not allow fear to stand in our way. Universal suffrage on a common voters' role in a united democratic and nonracial South Africa is the only way to peace and racial harmony.

In conclusion, I wish to quote my own words during my trial in 1964. They are true today as they were then: "I have fought against white domination and I have fought against black domination. I have cherished the ideal of a democratic and free society in which all persons live together in harmony and with equal opportunities. It is an ideal which I hope to live for and to achieve. But if needs be, it is an ideal for which I am prepared to die."

---

[12] Mandela, who had a stormy relationship with de Klerk during subsequent negotiations, quickly retracted this assessment.

▶ **MANDELA'S TINY FOUR-ROOM HOUSE** in Soweto's suburb of Orlando soon became the busiest patch of real estate in South Africa. An endless stream of visitors from every section of society arrived at all times of day and night to pay their respects. On one occasion a delegation of family and tribal elders arrived from Transkei with a cow, which was slaughtered on his tiny front lawn to celebrate his freedom. But it was also here that political leaders, diplomats, and foreign dignitaries would arrive to pay their respects. Here, on the day after his release from prison, Mandela addresses a crowd outside his house with Cyril Ramaphosa, a senior ANC leader (far left), and Andrew Mlangeni, a fellow Robben Island prisoner (third from left).

Photograph by Anne Day

▲ **WAITING FOR MANDELA:** Mandela, at peace with himself and confident of his goals after twenty-seven years of contemplation and strategizing, had a natural affinity with children. They would wait at the gate of his tiny house in Vilakazi Street until he got home and greeted them. It was a source of deep sadness to Mandela that his life in prison, in court, and on the run had prevented him from being more of a father to his own children. When he stepped down as president in 1999, he had more time with his daughters and grandchildren.

Photograph by Anne Day

It was a source of deep sadness to Mandela that his life in prison, in court, and on the run had prevented him from being more of a father to his own children.

▼ **FOLLOWING PAGES:** Mandela loved children and lost no opportunity to share moments of joy with them after his release from prison in February 1990. But he also had a stern side, and he constantly stressed the importance of getting a good education and working hard in school. In the first years after his release, Mandela launched the Nelson Mandela Children's Fund after a moving personal encounter with homeless children in Cape Town who came to him to explain their plight. The fund has since collected more than $100 million, and Mandela donated a third of his presidential salary to the fund during his five years in office.

Photograph by Louise Gubb

Pop star Brenda Fassie visited Mandela shortly after his release from prison. Fourteen years later, Mandela would sit in vigil at her bedside as she died from a cocaine overdose.

▶ **I LOVE YOU NELSON:** Brenda Fassie, one of South Africa's most successful female pop stars, hugs Mandela with her trademark passion after his release from jail in February 1990. Fassie, who died from a drug overdose in 2004 at the age of thirty-nine, was known as the Queen of African Pop. She composed a song dedicated to Mandela that she sang to him at a live performance in Johannesburg. Both Mandela and his wife, Winnie, went to visit her in the hospital before her death. Mandela, who was transfixed by the rhythmic music of southern Africa, developed what became known as the Madiba Jive, which enabled him to dance freely with the top half of his body while going easy on his hips and legs. Madiba is an honorary title for leaders of Mandela's tribal clan, and in South Africa, Mandela is widely known by that name.

Photograph by Louise Gubb

◀ **RAINBOW CONCERT:** After Mandela's release, a wave of euphoria followed him wherever he went, both at home and abroad. It was during this period that Desmond Tutu, the archbishop of Cape Town, described South Africa as the Rainbow Nation to capture its cultural and ethnic diversity and the fact that a nonracial majority was united in supporting Mandela's vision for the country. The negotiated settlement that preceded the first democratic elections in 1994 was often described as a miracle in the same spirit. But the first years of democracy in South Africa have shown that the socioeconomic fault lines will take generations to overcome and that race is still a dominant factor in South African society.

Photograph by Lisa Trocchi

▼ **FOLLOWING PAGES:** Mandela and Archbishop Desmond Tutu developed a relationship of mutual respect that has few equals in the history of freedom struggles. The archbishop insisted that he would act as the voice of the voiceless when the anti-apartheid leadership was jailed, outlawed, and harassed, but that once the "true leaders" were free he would take a backseat. Archbishop Tutu's leadership of peaceful public protests in the months leading to Mandela's release were crucial in easing the transition from apartheid to democracy. His intervention in the public burnings of suspected collaborators by anti-apartheid mobs at the height of the conflict demonstrated courage and integrity. Tutu has been true to his commitment to stand aside for the movement's leaders, but he has never lost his voice on behalf of the poor nor blunted his sharp criticisms of official greed and insensitivity.

Photograph by David Turnley

▶ **THANK YOU BRITAIN:** Mandela acknowledges the crowd at a Wembley Stadium concert in April 1990 that celebrated his release from jail earlier that same year. Held in June 1988, the first Free Mandela concert was a seminal global event that transformed the image of the ANC and bestowed iconic status on Mandela in the international arena. Mandela had an ambivalent relationship with Britain as the former colonial power, but he and the ANC leadership felt eternal gratitude to the British people, whose solidarity with the victims of apartheid changed the policy of the British government and spawned a global anti-apartheid campaign that built an unstoppable momentum.

Photograph by Dominique Albert

Mandela was devoted to his mother and deeply affected by her death.

◀ **THE RIGHT-HAND HOUSE:** In May 1990, three months after his release from jail, Mandela said a prayer over his mother's grave, and other relatives' graves, in Qunu, the nearest town in the Transkei to his birthplace in the tiny village of Mvezo. In line with Xhosa custom at the time, Mandela's father had four wives. Mandela's mother, Nosekeni Fanny, was the "right-hand wife," and Mandela was the eldest son of the "right-hand house." Mandela was devoted to his mother and was deeply affected by her death in 1968 while he was in jail. After his release from prison, Mandela always maintained a home in Qunu, and he and his third wife, Graça Machel, frequently stayed there.

Photograph by Louise Gubb

MADIBA GOES GAGA: In South Africa, Mandela is widely referred to as Madiba, an honorary title for leaders of his tribal clan. Here, during his first visit to his ancestral home in the Transkei in three decades, Madiba meets his grandson Bambatha;

Mandela has an impressive array of grandchildren and great-grandchildren, and his annual Christmas parties for hundreds of children in the vicinity of Qunu are legendary. He has also held numerous family reunions at his home in Johannesburg.

Photographs by Louise Gubb

◀ **MANDELA AND DE KLERK:** Mandela and the last apartheid state president, F. W. de Klerk, led their respective constituencies to a historic peace settlement, but it was only through strong leadership that they persuaded their followers to reach out to each other rather than risk mutual destruction. They were not natural allies, and the tension was usually written on their faces as they tackled compromises and made commitments. On one occasion in the negotiating process, Mandela publicly reprimanded de Klerk for double-crossing him on a mutual agreement to suspend violence by the state and the ANC. De Klerk never fully recovered from this diminution of his stature.

Photograph by Louise Gubb

▼ **FOLLOWING PAGES:** Mandela surveys America from above with the help of a Trump Airlines pilot on his first visit to the United States in June 1990. The visit was a triumph. It included a ticker-tape parade in New York, an address to the United Nations, an address to a joint session of the U.S. Congress, and a meeting with the first President Bush at the White House. Despite his life of service to the community, Mandela was always comfortable in the company of powerful and wealthy celebrities, and he was never shy about accepting their hospitality.

Photograph by David Turnley

Mandela held the United Nations in the highest regard for the strong stand it had taken against apartheid.

▶ **MANDELA AT THE U.N.:** Mandela acknowledges rapturous applause at the United Nations in New York in June 1990, when he called on member countries to maintain sanctions against South Africa until apartheid was abolished. Mandela held the United Nations in the highest regard for the strong stand it had taken against apartheid in all its councils and for the creation of institutions such as the U.N. Special Committee Against Apartheid. It was in the U.N. General Assembly that African and Asian solidarity ensured a clear majority to end all forms of collaboration with South Africa.

Photograph by Don Emmert

Mandela was always keen to meet resistance leaders and those who had taken a clear moral stand on issues.

▶ **CIVIL RIGHTS:** During their visit to the United States in June 1990, Nelson and Winnie Mandela met the American civil rights pioneer Rosa Parks in Detroit, Michigan. Mandela was always keen to meet resistance leaders and those who had taken a clear moral stand on issues. He saw a close connection between the anti-apartheid struggle in South Africa and the civil rights struggle in the United States.

Photograph by David Turnley

PEACE CHEMISTRY: While there was clearly a degree of personal chemistry between Mandela and President F. W. de Klerk, the two leaders had to be constantly mindful of how their body language would be received by their respective constituencies. There were complex undercurrents at work at the signing of this peace accord between the three major leaders in September 1991. The epicenter of the conflict was the violence that had erupted between Zulu supporters of the ANC and loyalists swearing allegiance to Zulu Chief Mangosuthu Buthelezi's more traditionalist Inkatha Freedom Party. Tensions between de Klerk and Mandela, which focused on whether de Klerk was doing enough to rein in his security forces or whether he was turning a blind eye to a shadowy pro-apartheid third force, were subsumed on this occasion by the presence of Chief Buthelezi, who was seen as exploiting the intra-Zulu violence to undermine the emerging political settlement. Buthelezi hinted that the Zulu-dominated KwaZulu Natal province might secede from South Africa unless his demands for partial autonomy were met. At this meeting, attempts by both de Klerk and Mandela to shake hands with him publicly were thwarted by a sulking Buthelezi.

Photographs by Louise Gubb

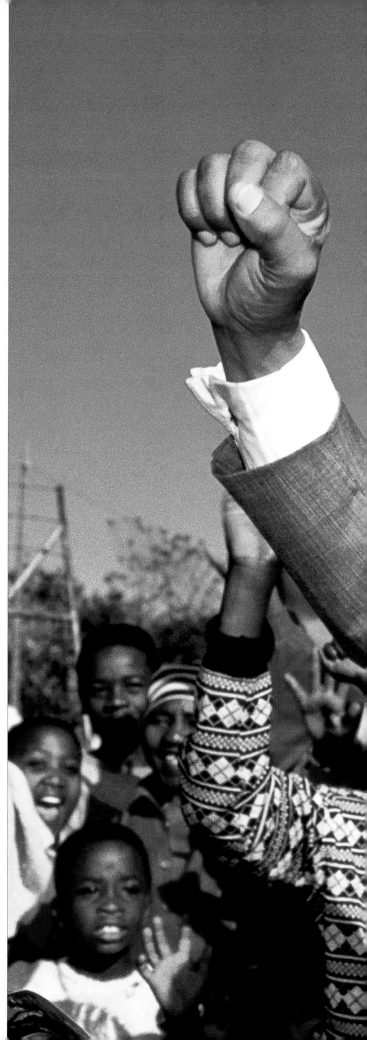

The first time Mandela urged a rally of young people to throw their weapons into the sea, he met with a mixed reaction.

▶ **POWER TO YOUR STUDIES:** In the period between his release in February 1990 and becoming the first black president of South Africa in 1994, Mandela traveled the length and breadth of the country to urge an end to the violence that threatened a political settlement, particularly in KwaZulu Natal province and in Johannesburg and its industrial satellites. The first time he urged a rally of mainly young people to throw their weapons into the sea, he met with a mixed reaction from the crowd. Here he wins acknowledgment from a group of students at a school near Johannesburg with a power salute, and then urges them to concentrate on their studies.

Photograph by Louise Gubb

◀ **STUDY IN BLACK AND WHITE:** Mandela made a point of being as inclusive as possible when inspiring South Africans to support his vision of a nonracial and democratic South Africa. The expressions on the faces of these boys at a mainly white school reflect the concern of those brought up to fear black South Africans. The expression of the black pupil on the right captures the moment at which black hopes overtook white fears before the country's first democratic elections in 1994. During this period, Mandela went to great lengths to reassure whites that their futures would be secure under a black majority government.

Photograph by Louise Gubb

▼ **FOLLOWING PAGES:** Mandela, wearing a flower garland and hat denoting the Hindu religion, shakes hands with religious leaders in 1993 while campaigning to become the country's first black president. Although Mandela seldom addressed the subject of religion in public, he disclosed in a long interview with this writer in 2000 that religion had had a major influence on his life. Under a government that had little if any interest in the quality of education for black South Africans, Mandela attended a rural school run by Christian missionaries and saw religion as a force for development. "Religion has had a tremendous influence on my own life," he said. "From Grade one up to university, our education was provided by religious institutions."

Photograph by Louise Gubb

◀ **STANDING OUT IN A CROWD:** Mandela is surrounded by supporters in the densely populated black township of Khayelit-sha, near Cape Town, in 1993 while campaigning to take part in the country's first democratic elections in 1994. Both the ANC and the country's white leaders, who needed Mandela to persuade blacks to support the political compromise, lived in fear that he would be assassinated. On countless occasions he would have been an easy target for a sniper or lone right-wing gunman, such as the one who brought the country to the brink of a violent catastrophe in April 1993 by killing ANC leader Chris Hani. At that time, Mandela had to muster all his reserves of leadership to rescue the negotiating process.

Photograph by Louise Gubb

▲ PAS DE DEUX: Mandela and F. W. de Klerk display the Nobel Peace Prizes they received for leading negotiations that achieved a peaceful end to four decades of apartheid in South Africa. Controversy followed as to whether it was right to equate the contributions of Mandela and de Klerk. De Klerk continued to support the settlement by assuming the role of second deputy to Mandela in a unity government, but he later withdrew from the government and retired from politics.

Photograph by Yves Forestier

◀ VIVA MADIBA: Archbishop Desmond Tutu, who was crucial in preparing the ground for the release of Mandela and other anti-apartheid leaders, characteristically rubs his hands with glee as he watches Mandela and South African President F. W. de Klerk receive the Nobel Peace Prize in Oslo, Norway, in 1993 for their role in negotiating a peaceful settlement in South Africa. Archbishop Tutu had won the same prize a decade earlier, in 1984, for his work in moderating violent resistance to apartheid across the country. Tutu never wavered in his personal commitment to peace, but he respected the ANC's decision to resort to armed struggle when all avenues of peaceful protest were outlawed.

Photograph by Louise Gubb

MORE PRECIOUS THAN DIAMONDS

Oslo, Norway, December 10, 1993

Nelson Mandela delivered this speech upon acceptance of the Nobel Peace Prize.[1]

Your Majesty the King[2], Your Royal Highness, Honorable Prime Minister Madame Gro Brundtland,[3] ministers, members of Parliament and ambassadors, esteemed members of the Norwegian Nobel Committee, fellow laureate Mr. F. W. de Klerk, distinguished guests, friends, ladies and gentlemen:

I am indeed truly humbled to be standing here today to receive this year's Nobel Peace Prize.

I extend my heartfelt thanks to the Norwegian Nobel Committee for elevating us to the status of Nobel Peace Prize winners.

I would also like to take this opportunity to congratulate my compatriot and fellow laureate, State President F. W. de Klerk, on his receipt of this high honor. Together, we join two distinguished South Africans, the late Chief

---

[1] This speech is reproduced in its entirety. Footnotes have been added to explain certain historical references, and words have been added in brackets [ ] for the same purpose. Spelling and punctuation have been Americanized. This speech, and many others by Mandela, can be found at www.anc.org.za. ("More Precious Than Diamonds" is not the original title of the speech.)

[2] King Harald V of Norway.

[3] The prime minister of Norway (1986–89 and 1990–96).

Albert Luthuli[4] and His Grace Archbishop Desmond Tutu,[5] to whose seminal contributions to the peaceful struggle against the evil system of apartheid you paid well-deserved tribute by awarding them the Nobel Peace Prize.

It will not be presumptuous of us if we also add, among our predecessors, the name of another outstanding Nobel Peace Prize winner, the late African American statesman and internationalist, the Reverend Martin Luther King Jr.

He, too, grappled with, and died in, the effort to make a contribution to the just solution of the same great issues of the day which we have had to face as South Africans. We speak here of the challenge of the dichotomies of war and peace, violence and nonviolence, racism and human dignity, oppression and repression, liberty and human rights, poverty and freedom from want.

These countless human beings had the nobility of spirit to stand in the path of tyranny and injustice without seeking selfish gain.

We stand here today as nothing more than a representative of the millions of our people who dared to rise up against a social system whose very essence is war, violence, racism, oppression, repression, and the impoverishment of an entire people. I am also here today as a representative of the millions of people across the globe, the anti-apartheid movement, the governments and organizations that joined with us, not to fight against South Africa as a country or any of its peoples, but to oppose an inhuman system and sue for a speedy end to the apartheid crime against humanity.

These countless human beings, both inside and outside our country, had the nobility of spirit to stand in the path of tyranny and injustice without seeking selfish gain. They recognized that an injury to one is an injury to

[4] A Zulu chieftain who received the 1960 Nobel Peace Prize for his role in the nonviolent struggle against apartheid.

[5] The Anglican archbishop of Cape Town who received the 1984 Nobel Peace Prize for his long battle to achieve a nonviolent end to apartheid.

all, and therefore acted together in defense of justice and common human decency. Because of their courage and persistence for many years, we can, today, even set the dates when all humanity will join together to celebrate one of the outstanding human victories of our century. When that moment comes, we shall, together, rejoice in a common victory over racism, apartheid, and white minority rule.

At the southern tip of the continent of Africa, a rich reward is in the making, an invaluable gift is in the preparation.

That triumph will finally bring to a close a history of five hundred years of African colonization that began with the establishment of the Portuguese empire [in Africa]. Thus, it will mark a great step forward in history and also serve as a common pledge of the peoples of the world to fight racism wherever it occurs and whatever guise it assumes.

At the southern tip of the continent of Africa, a rich reward is in the making, an invaluable gift is in the preparation, for those who suffered in the name of all humanity when they sacrificed everything for liberty, peace, human dignity, and human fulfillment. This reward will not be measured in money. Nor can it be reckoned in the collective price of the rare metals and precious stones that rest in the bowels of the African soil we tread in the footsteps of our ancestors.

It will and must be measured by the happiness and welfare of the children, at once the most vulnerable citizens in any society and the greatest of our treasures. The children must, at last, play in the open veld,[6] no longer tortured by the pangs of hunger or ravaged by disease or threatened with the scourge of ignorance, molestation, and abuse, and no longer required to engage in deeds whose gravity exceeds the demands of their tender years. In front of

---

[6] The flat grasslands of South Africa.

this distinguished audience, we commit the new South Africa to the relentless pursuit of the purposes defined in the World Declaration on the Survival, Protection and Development of Children.

The reward of which we have spoken will, and must also be, measured by the happiness and welfare of the mothers and fathers of these children, who must walk the earth without fear of being robbed, killed for political or material profit, or spat upon because they are beggars.

They too must be relieved of the heavy burden of despair which they carry in their hearts, born of hunger, homelessness, and unemployment.

The value of that gift to all who have suffered will, and must be, measured by the happiness and welfare of all the people of our country, who will have torn down the inhuman walls that divide them. These great masses will have turned their backs on the grave insult to human dignity which

We will have created a society which recognizes that all people are born equal with each entitled, in equal measure, to life, liberty, prosperity, and human rights.

described some as masters and others as servants, and transformed each into a predator whose survival depended on the destruction of the other.

The value of our shared reward will and must be measured by the joyful peace which will triumph, because the common humanity that bonds both black and white into one human race will have said to each one of us that we shall all live like the children of paradise.

Thus shall we live, because we will have created a society which recognizes that all people are born equal with each entitled, in equal measure, to life, liberty, prosperity, human rights, and good governance. Such a society should never allow again that there should be prisoners of conscience, nor that any person's human rights should be violated. Neither should it ever happen that once more the avenues to peaceful change are blocked by usurpers who seek to take power away from the people in pursuit of their own ignoble purposes.

In relation to these matters, we appeal to those who govern Burma that they release our fellow Nobel Peace Prize laureate Aung San Suu Kyi, and engage her and those she represents in serious dialogue, for the benefit of all the people of Burma. We pray that those who have the power to do so will, without further delay, permit that she uses her talents and energies for the greater good of the people of her country and humanity as a whole.

Let us all prove Martin Luther King Jr. correct when he said that humanity can no longer be tragically bound to the starless midnight of racism and war.

Far from the rough and tumble of the politics of our own country, I would like to take this opportunity to join the Norwegian Nobel Committee and pay tribute to my joint laureate, Mr. F. W. de Klerk. He had the courage to admit that a terrible wrong had been done to our country and people through the imposition of the system of apartheid. He had the foresight to understand and accept that all the people of South Africa must, through negotiations and as equal participants in the process, together determine what they want to make of their future.

But there are still some within our country who wrongly believe they can make a contribution to the cause of justice and peace by clinging to the shibboleths that have been proved to spell nothing but disaster. It remains our hope that these, too, will be blessed with sufficient reason to realize that history will not be denied and that the new society cannot be created by reproducing the repugnant past, however refined or enticingly repackaged.

We live with the hope that as she battles to remake herself, South Africa will be like a microcosm of the new world that is striving to be born. This must be a world of democracy and respect for human rights, a world freed from the horrors of poverty, hunger, deprivation, and ignorance, relieved of the threat and the scourge of civil wars and external aggression, and unburdened of the great tragedy of millions forced to become refugees. The processes in which South Africa and southern Africa as a whole are engaged, beckon and urge us all that we take this tide at the flood and make of this region a living example of what all people of conscience would like the world to be.

We do not believe that this Nobel Peace Prize is intended as a commendation for matters that have happened and passed. We hear the voices which say that it is an appeal from all those, throughout the universe, who sought an end to the system of apartheid. We understand their call, that we devote what remains of our lives to the use of our country's unique and painful experience to demonstrate, in practice, that the normal condition for human existence is democracy, justice, peace, nonracism, nonsexism, prosperity for everybody, a healthy environment, and equality and solidarity among the peoples.

Moved by that appeal and inspired by the eminence you have thrust upon us, we undertake that we too will do what we can to contribute to the renewal of our world so that none should, in future, be described as the wretched of the earth.

Let it never be said by future generations that indifference, cynicism, or selfishness made us fail to live up to the ideals of humanism which the Nobel Peace Prize encapsulates.

Let the strivings of us all prove Martin Luther King Jr. to have been correct when he said that humanity can no longer be tragically bound to the starless midnight of racism and war.

Let the efforts of us all prove that he was not a mere dreamer when he spoke of the beauty of genuine brotherhood and peace being more precious than diamonds or silver or gold.

Let a new age dawn!

▶ BACK TO HIS ROOTS: Mandela returns to his birthplace in rural Transkei, near the town of Qunu, before the country's first democratic elections in 1994. He is standing in front of a traditional Xhosa house made of mud, straw, and a thatched roof. His father, a minor royal, died when he was only five years old, and Mandela was placed under the custodianship of the regent Xhosa king, Jongintaba Dalindyebo. Mandela was groomed to become an advisor to Jongintaba's son Justice. But when he was set up for an arranged marriage in the Xhosa tribal custom, Mandela fled the Transkei for Johannesburg.

Photograph by David Turnley

◀ SUIT-AND-TIE CAMPAIGNER: Mandela campaigns in a suit and tie prior to the 1994 presidential election. Today in South Africa, it is difficult to find people wearing suits and ties, even in the business district of Johannesburg or the parliamentary chambers. Mandela, always known for his sartorial prowess, had much to do with ushering in a more informal style with his colorful and loose-fitting Madiba shirts, which became one of his trademarks as president; he even wore them to state banquets.

Photograph by David Turnley

▼ FOLLOWING PAGES: Mandela attends a campaign rally in the Xhosa rural heartland of Transkei, on South Africa's eastern seaboard. The Transkei was one of several designated black "homelands," known as Bantustans. The designation of "independent" black states was an ill-fated attempt to ensure that blacks could not outvote whites in elections in "white" South Africa. The scheme was formally abandoned with the drawing up of a new interim constitution, which was endorsed in the country's first democratic elections in 1994.

Photograph by David Turnley

Mandela was the son of a minor Xhosa royal. Upon his father's death, he became a ward of the regent Xhosa king, Jongintaba Dalindyebo.

◄ **MADIBA THE CHIEF:** Mandela wears tribal regalia, including a leopard-skin cloak, while campaigning in Ciskei during the country's first democratic elections in 1994. Ciskei was one of a handful of "independent" homelands that were an integral part of apartheid. The smaller of the two Xhosa homelands, it has a somewhat bizarre history: Colonel Oupa Gqozo staged a coup against his brother, the leader of Ciskei, four weeks after Mandela was freed, but he later resigned.

Photograph by Peter Turnley

After twenty-seven years behind bars, Mandela was a natural on the campaign trail.

◄ **CAMPAIGN TRAIL:** After twenty-seven years behind bars, and with the country hanging on his every word, Mandela was a natural on the campaign trail. He breathed new life into the ANC and became one of the world's most successful fundraisers. Everyone wanted to bask in the warmth of his magic smile. As he was paraded on the rooftops of limousines, in pickups, and on podiums, Mandela walked the talk. What you saw was what you got: a legend who was also a flesh-and-blood man that you could reach out and touch.

Photograph by Peter Turnley

▶ **FLYING HIGH:** As he blazed a campaign trail unlike anything seen before in South Africa, Mandela was having a ball. When the election campaign reached a crescendo in the first months of 1994, the country united behind one extraordinary man who had discovered exactly who he was and where he was going. Mandela had had twenty-seven years to sort his baggage and put it in the closet. Now he was traveling light.

Photograph by Peter Turnley

▼ **FOLLOWING PAGES:** In the run-up to South Africa's first democratic elections in 1994, Mandela's face—framed in the ANC colors of black, green, and yellow—smiled from every lamppost, billboard, and tree. Within months of the election, these same posters had become collector's items and were being exported, sold, and auctioned. Everything Madiba touched was magic. This supporter insures that the local Mandela posters will not end up in the trash can.

Photograph by David Turnley

In changing
himself, Mandela
changed the
course of history.

▶ **MIDDLE DISTANCE:** A pensive Mandela seems to be staring into the middle distance as he returns to the tiny cell in which he spent nineteen years and, in changing himself, changed the course of history. In an interview in 2000, after he stepped down as president, he told this writer that having twenty-seven years to think about one's own life—including the mistakes made—and having time to read the biographies of great people was a transformative experience. It taught him to respect even the most ordinary people, and that great problems destroy some people and make others stronger. "It is possible that if I had not gone to jail and been able to read and listen to the stories of many people... I might not have learned these things," he told me.

Photograph by Louise Gubb

▲ **MEMORY LANE:** On February 11, 1994, the fourth anniversary of Mandela's release, the president and six of his fellow prisoners return to the Robben Island lime quarry where they worked. From left: Dennis Goldberg, Andrew Mlangeni, Nelson Mandela, Ahmed Kathrada, and Walter Sisulu, all fellow defendants at the Treason Trial. On the far right is Wilton Mkwayi, who was arrested after the Rivonia Trial and was tried and convicted separately on similar charges. Mandela, who turned down conditional release several times, insisted that his colleagues all be released before he would accept freedom.

▶ **LOOKING BACK:** Mandela revisits the tiny cell where he was imprisoned for nineteen years and allows himself a whimsical smile in the knowledge that he not only transcended the experience, but also negotiated both himself and his people out of imprisonment. Mandela always treated the prison guards and officers with respect and in some cases formed warm personal relationships that survived his release. His frequent letters petitioning prison authorities for more rights bore the unmistakable moral authority that became his hallmark.

Photographs by Louise Gubb

▶ **VOTE OF THANKS:** While campaigning for the presidency in the rural areas of the Eastern Cape where he grew up, Mandela, wearing traditional dress, stops his convoy to thank soldiers of the South African Defence Force. The SADF, which served the apartheid government for forty years, played a critical role in keeping the peace during the country's first democratic elections in April 1994. Mandela knew only too well that the toughest part of the power-sharing negotiations had been the status of the armed forces and how they would be reconstituted to include their former enemies, the military wing of the ANC and other liberation armies. The symbolic moment of change came on the day of his inauguration, May 10, 1994, when President Mandela saluted the flypast of the South African Air Force.

Photograph by Andrew Lichtenstein

▲ **BALLOT POWER:** When voting day dawned on April 27, 1994, South Africans got their first glimpse of the new South Africa as millions of people of all races joined long voting lines across the country. Some queues were more than a half mile (about a kilometer) long and formed switchbacks to fit into confined spaces. Some people queued all day, and nobody who voted was quite the same again. For the first time in the country's history, all of its citizens had participated in a mass activity together, as equals. Whatever challenges lay ahead—and there would be many—South Africans had seen the future, and it worked.

Photographs by David Brauchli

▼ **FOLLOWING PAGES:** Voters in South Africa's first democratic elections in 1994 queue patiently in the sun to cast a ballot for the very first time. Democracy took on a new meaning as ordinary South Africans all across the country participated in choosing their government. This photograph was taken in rural Transkei, close to where Mandela grew up.

Photograph by Peter Turnley

It was a fitting moment of triumph in Mandela's long walk to freedom.

▶ **THE DECISIVE MOMENT:** Nelson Mandela votes for the first time in his life on April 27, 1994. It was the first election open to all races after the abolition of apartheid, the system that Mandela had spent his lifetime resisting and, ultimately, had overthrown through his leadership, moral authority, and personal courage. For Mandela, who wore one of his trademark loose-hanging Madiba shirts and his magic Madiba smile, casting his ballot was a fitting moment of triumph in his long walk to freedom. It was a moment that many South Africans thought they would never live to see, and the world watched in awe.

Photograph by Louise Gubb

When Mandela
signed his name,
he officially
became the first
president of the
newly democratic
South Africa.

◀ **FREE AT LAST:** Former President F. W. de Klerk and his
wife, Marike, applaud as President Nelson Rolihlahla Mandela
signs the register after his inauguration as president of South
Africa on May 19, 1994. Mandela and de Klerk won a joint Nobel Peace Prize for their contribution to a peaceful settlement
of South Africa's seemingly intractable race problem. Mandela
stood down after his first term in office in 1999 to make way
for his successor, Thabo Mbeki. In May 2009, Jacob Zuma became the third president of the democratic South Africa and
the first Zulu president.

Photograph by Louise Gubb

INAUGURAL ADDRESS OF THE PRESIDENT OF THE DEMOCRATIC REPUBLIC OF SOUTH AFRICA

Pretoria, South Africa, May 10, 1994[1]

Your majesties, your highnesses, distinguished guests, comrades and friends:

Today, all of us do, by our presence here, and by our celebrations in other parts of our country and the world, confer glory and hope to newborn liberty. Out of the experience of an extraordinary human disaster that lasted too long, must be born a society of which all humanity will be proud.

Our daily deeds as ordinary South Africans must produce an actual South African reality that will reinforce humanity's belief in justice, strengthen its confidence in the nobility of the human soul, and sustain all our hopes for a glorious life for all. All this we owe both to ourselves and to the peoples of the world who are so well represented here today.

To my compatriots, I have no hesitation in saying that each one of us is as intimately attached to the soil of this beautiful country as the famous jacaranda trees of Pretoria and the mimosa trees of the bushveld.[2] Each time one of us

---

[1] This speech is reproduced in its entirety. Footnotes have been added to explain certain historical references, and words have been added in brackets [ ] for the same purpose. Spelling and punctuation have been Americanized. This speech, and many others by Mandela, can be found at www.anc.org.za.

[2] The grasslands of South Africa; similar to the Australian use of the word "outback."

touches the soil of this land, we feel a sense of personal renewal. The national mood changes as the seasons change. We are moved by a sense of joy and exhilaration when the grass turns green and the flowers bloom.

That spiritual and physical oneness we all share with this common homeland explains the depth of the pain we all carried in our hearts as we saw our country tear itself apart in a terrible conflict. And as we saw it spurned, outlawed, and isolated by the peoples of the world, precisely because it has become the universal base of the pernicious ideology and practice of racism and racial oppression.

We, the people of South Africa, feel fulfilled that humanity has taken us back into its bosom, that we, who

▲ **HAND ON HEART:** President Mandela and his two deputies, Thabo Mbeki (left) and F. W. de Klerk (right), stand at attention while the military band plays the national anthem at the inauguration of the country's first black president on May 10, 1994. Mandela and Mbeki are saluting during the singing of the new national anthem, a hybrid of the old Afrikaner anthem "Die Stem van Suid-Afrika" ("The Call of South Africa") and the southern African anthem "Nkosi Sikelel' iAfrika" ("God Bless Africa").

Photograph by Louise Gubb

were outlaws not so long ago, have today been given the rare privilege to be host to the nations of the world on our own soil.

We thank all our distinguished international guests for having come to take possession with the people of our country of what is, after all, a common victory for justice, for peace, for human dignity. We trust that you will continue to stand by us as we tackle the challenges of building peace, prosperity, nonsexism, nonracialism, and democracy.

We have, at last, achieved our political emancipation. We commit ourselves to the construction of a complete, just, and lasting peace.

We deeply appreciate the role that the masses of our people and their political mass democratic, religious, women, youth, business, traditional, and other leaders have played to bring about this conclusion. Not least among them is my second deputy president, the Honorable F. W. de Klerk.

We would also like to pay tribute to our security forces, in all their ranks, for the distinguished role they have played in securing our first democratic elections and the transition to democracy, from bloodthirsty forces which still refuse to see the light.

The time for the healing of the wounds has come.

The moment to bridge the chasms that divide us has come.

The time to build is upon us.

We have, at last, achieved our political emancipation. We pledge ourselves to liberate all our people from the continuing bondage of poverty, deprivation, suffering, gender and other discrimination.

We succeeded to take our last steps to freedom in conditions of relative peace. We commit ourselves to the construction of a complete, just, and lasting peace.

We have triumphed in the effort to implant hope in the breasts of the millions of our people. We enter into a covenant that we shall build the society in which all South Africans, both black and white, will be able to walk tall, without any fear in their hearts, assured of their inalienable right to human dignity—a rainbow nation at peace with itself and the world.

As a token of its commitment to the renewal of our country, the new Interim Government of National Unity will, as a matter of urgency, address the issue of amnesty for various categories of our people who are currently serving terms of imprisonment.

We dedicate this day to all the heroes and heroines in this country and the rest of the world who sacrificed in many ways and surrendered their lives so that we could be free.

Their dreams have become reality. Freedom is their reward.

We are both humbled and elevated by the honor and privilege that you, the people of South Africa, have bestowed on us, as the first president of a united, democratic, nonracial and nonsexist government.

We understand it still that there is no easy road to freedom. We know it well that none of us acting alone can achieve success. We must therefore act together as a united people, for national reconciliation, for nation building, for the birth of a new world.

Let there be justice for all.

Let there be peace for all.

Let there be work, bread, water, and salt for all.

Let each know that for each the body, the mind, and the soul have been freed to fulfill themselves.

Never, never, and never again shall it be that this beautiful land will again experience the oppression of one by another and suffer the indignity of being the skunk of the world.

Let freedom reign.

The sun shall never set on so glorious a human achievement!

God bless Africa!

▶ **RUGBY RESUMED:** President Mandela, saluting during the singing of the new national anthem, is flanked by Deputy President F. W. de Klerk in June 1994 at the first rugby game to be played after the global boycott of sport with South Africa was lifted. A match against England played in Pretoria, the game was an important symbolic act for white South Africans and a tangible benefit of democracy. Francois Pienaar—captain of the Springboks, the South African team—is standing behind Mr. de Klerk at the extreme right. Pienaar was destined to play a historic role in cementing the transition to democracy at the Rugby World Cup the following year.

Photograph by Louise Gubb

IN WHAT AUTHOR JOHN CARLIN, in *Playing the Enemy*, described as the "most improbable exercise in mass seduction ever seen," President Mandela, wearing a green and gold Springbok rugby jersey, congratulates South African rugby captain Francois Pienaar after the Springboks beat the New Zealand All Blacks 15-12 to win the 1995 Rugby World Cup. The moment, which transcended sport, marked the turning point at which whites embraced the ANC government led by Mandela as their own. The Springboks credited their narrow victory, at least in part, to Mandela's support. "We didn't have 62,000 fans behind us. We had 43 million South Africans," Pienaar said in a television interview. The exchange between the two after the match was memorable: "Francois, thank you very much for what you have done for our country," said Mandela. "No, Mr. President," Pienaar replied. "Thank *you* very much for what *you* have done for our country."

Photograph Above by Louise Gubb

Mandela's 1994 visit to the United States was his first as head of state.

◄ **PRESIDENT MANDELA ACKNOWLEDGES** thunderous applause while delivering remarks to a joint session of the U.S. Congress in Washington, D.C., on October 6, 1994. Applauding Mandela against the backdrop of the Stars and Stripes are Vice President Al Gore (left) and Speaker of the House Tom Foley. The visit to the United States was Mandela's first as head of state. He had received one of the largest ticker-tape parade welcomes in the history of New York City when he visited the country after his release in February 1990.

Photograph by Greg Newton

Mandela and the queen of England were on a first-name basis, and there appeared to be genuine warmth between them.

▶ **ROYALTY UNITED:** Smiling broadly, quite uncharacteristic in a formal photograph, Queen Elizabeth II is seen with President Mandela, a minor Xhosa royal himself, at London's Dorchester Hotel, where he hosted a banquet during his state visit to Britain in July 1996, on the eve of his seventy-eighth birthday. Mandela was completely comfortable in the queen's presence and struck up a personal relationship with her. He would call from time to time to inquire after the family and was particularly concerned about the welfare of Princess Diana's sons, Princes William and Harry, after Diana's death.

Mandela developed long friendships with two warders who had him under their charge on Robben Island.

◀ **JAILER AND THE JAILED:** Mandela shares a joke with one of his former prison guards, Warrant Officer Swart, during a visit to the house at Victor Verster Prison in Paarl, near Cape Town, where Mandela lived during the last two years of his incarceration. Swart was his cook and valet during this period, a far cry from the time when Mandela was breaking rocks on Robben Island. Mandela had a constant stream of visitors—colleagues from the internal wing of the ANC as well as other prominent figures—who helped prepare him for life on the outside.

Photograph by Louise Gubb

Mandela loved receiving celebrities he had heard about in prison, apparently unaware that he was as famous as they were.

▶ **THE PRESIDENT AND THE PRINCESS:** President Mandela receives Diana, Princess of Wales, in Cape Town in May 1997, shortly before her death in a tragic auto accident in Paris. Mandela, always comfortable in the presence of celebrities, was clearly delighted with the princess, and there was an immediate and natural rapport between them. They shared a passion for children and for finding ways to make the world a better place.

▲ **PRESIDENTS BEHIND BARS:** U.S. President Bill Clinton and President Nelson Mandela look out through the bars of the jail cell that was Mandela's window on the world for nineteen years. Clinton was on a state visit to South Africa in 1998. The two presidents developed a close relationship, and Mandela stood solidly by Clinton throughout the Monica Lewinsky scandal. In an interview in the *Guardian* before the publication of his biography, Clinton acknowledged that Mandela's friendship and counsel had helped him get through the Lewinsky matter. "Mandela told me he forgave his oppressors because if he didn't they would have destroyed him," Clinton said. The exchange took place here, in Mandela's old cell.

Photograph by Scott Applewhite

Clinton said to an interviewer, "Mandela told me he forgave his oppressors because if he didn't they would have destroyed him."

Mandela's face lit up like a teenager's as he told me about Graça, and then showed me pictures of her.

▶ **LOVERS AT SEA:** Mandela and his third wife, Graça Machel, share a joyous moment in their stateroom on the luxury ocean liner *Queen Elizabeth 2* in March 1998. The couple were married in July 1998 following a two-year courtship. This writer spent a long lunch at Mandela's house in 1996 hearing the details of his touching relationship with Graça and the compromise arrangement the couple had made whereby Graça would spend two weeks of every month in Mozambique, where she is a prominent public figure as a former first lady, and two weeks at Mandela's Johannesburg home or at the house in Qunu near his birthplace. His face lit up like a teenager's as he told their story, and then showed me pictures of her.

Photograph by Louise Gubb

It was as though he, too, wanted to know who this Nelson Mandela was.

◄ **NURTURE OR NATURE?** Nelson Mandela savors the wonder of life on a perfect spring day. The question that has always fascinated me is "Who is Nelson Mandela?" This writer was once alone with Mandela on his private jet to Durban for an election rally. He was tired and had his legs up and covered with a blanket. After gazing out the window for a time, he began to speak about himself with a sense of detachment. It was as though he, too, wanted to know who this Nelson Mandela was, and what would happen to him when he relinquished his post as president of the country and the ANC.

Photograph by Micheline Pelletier

◄ **OLD-TIME RELIGION:** Nelson Mandela meets Pope John Paul II in the Vatican during an official visit in June 1998. In December 1999, Mandela addressed a gathering of religious leaders from the world's major faiths in Cape Town, speaking publicly about his views on religion for the first time. "I appreciate the importance of religion," he said. Mandela said that real leaders were those who thought about the poor twenty-four hours a day and who knew in their hearts that poverty was the single biggest threat to society. "We have seen enough injustice, strife, division, suffering, and pain, and our capacity to be massively inhuman. But this gathering [of religious leaders] counters despairing cynicism and reaffirms the nobility of the human spirit."

Photograph by Franco Origlia

The Truth and Reconciliation Commission hearings drew large audiences, and the anger and emotion at the hearings were often audible and tangible.

▶ **FORGIVENESS:** Archbishop Desmond Tutu hands the records of the Truth and Reconciliation Commission, which he chaired, to President Mandela in October 1998, after nearly three years of hearings. The hearings granted amnesty to perpetrators of apartheid-era atrocities in exchange for disclosure. The archbishop shared the pain of the victims, who had to retell their stories, and broke down on several occasions. The hearings drew large audiences, and the anger and emotion were often audible and tangible. Mandela believed that reconciling with one's adversaries changed one fundamentally and made one a better person.

Photograph by Louise Gubb

BE MY VALENTINE: Mandela married Graça Machel, the widow of Mozambique's founding president, on his eightieth birthday in 1998. The first stirrings, according to Mandela, took place when they met at a memorial for Samora Machel, who died in a mysterious plane crash in Mozambique in 1986. Mandela and Graça saw each other again about a year later, at an academic investiture in Cape Town where Graça

received an honorary doctorate. "That's when I was really struck by what a gracious person she is," Madiba told friends at the time. Here they are doing what should be done on Valentine's Day.

Photographs by Louise Gubb

▲ **THE GURU AND THE GEEK:** Nelson Mandela and Bill Gates—two icons in their own lifetimes—applaud a speaker at a global health discussion in Seattle in December 1999, shortly after Mandela stepped down as South Africa's first black president. Gates, the co-founder of Microsoft, invited Mandela as a guest of the Bill & Melinda Gates Foundation, which had researched a vaccination for AIDS and considered nutrition as a factor in combating the disease. Mandela, who was later to clash with his successor over the South African government's AIDS policy, spent three days in Seattle talking to community leaders.

Photograph by Jeff Christensen

Mandela would later clash with his successor over the South African government's AIDS policy.

▶ **THE ESSENCE OF MANDELA:** "If you have an objective in life, then you want to concentrate on that and not engage in infighting with your enemies," Mandela told this writer in an interview shortly after stepping down as president. "You want to create an atmosphere where you can move everybody towards the goal you have set for yourself—as well as the collective [organization] for which you work. And, therefore, for all people who have found themselves in the position of being in jail and trying to transform society, forgiveness is natural because you have no time to be retaliative... You want to mobilize everybody to support your cause and the aims you have set for your life."

Photograph by Stephane Ruet

▲ **TWO REVOLUTIONARIES:** Mandela hugs Fidel Castro during a visit to Mandela's home in Houghton, a suburb of Johannesburg, in September 2001. Castro was in South Africa to attend the World Conference Against Racism. Mandela had no qualms about embracing leaders regarded as pariahs by the West, including Castro, PLO leader Yasser Arafat, Libyan President Muammar Gadhafi, and Ayatollah Khomeini of Iran.

Photograph by Chris Kotze

▲ **MUTUAL ADMIRATION SOCIETY:** Nelson Mandela throws his arm around the shoulders of popular U.S. talk show host Oprah Winfrey after they break the ground for her $40 million Leadership Academy for Girls in Henley-on-Klip, South Africa, in December 2002. They were two celebrities comfortable in each other's company, having struck up an immediate rapport when Mandela appeared on her show after his release from twenty-seven years in jail in February 1990. During remarks at the groundbreaking, Winfrey described Mandela as her hero and he called her a queen.

Photograph by Louise Gubb

46664: In November 2003, a host of artists from around the world staged a benefit concert in Cape Town for 46664, a global HIV/AIDS awareness and prevention campaign begun by the Nelson Mandela Foundation. The campaign was named after Mandela's prisoner number, and many celebrities, including entrepreneur Sir Richard Branson and musician Peter Gabriel, stenciled "46664" on their foreheads.

Photographs by Louise Gubb

The Xhosa king presented Mandela with the feather of the blue crane to mark his achievements.

► **AS A BOY, NELSON MANDELA** was assigned to the Xhosa regent Jongintaba Dalindyebo to be trained as a royal advisor. He ran away to Johannesburg rather than submit to an arranged marriage, and the rest is history. Here, Xhosa King Sigcau presents Mandela with the honor of *isithwalandwe*, the feather of the blue crane, to mark Mandela's royal lineage and his achievements. Mandela never lost touch with his tribal culture and network despite becoming a lawyer, an activist, and, eventually, the first president of a democratic South Africa.

Photograph by Louise Gubb

Mandela says, "Children are the rock on which our future will be built."

◄ **NELSON MANDELA IS CHARACTERISTICALLY AT EASE** with a group of schoolchildren during a week of activities to mark his eighty-eighth birthday in 2006. The Nelson Mandela Children's Fund, which Mandela founded in 1995, continues to support projects that benefit impoverished youth in South Africa.

▲ **WORLD LEADERS:** A frail but smiling Nelson Mandela, the first black president of South Africa, takes the arm of Kofi Annan, the first black African secretary-general of the United Nations, as Annan visits Johannesburg in July 2007 to deliver the fifth annual Nelson Mandela lecture. Other speakers in the series, presented by the Nelson Mandela Foundation, have included former U.S. President Bill Clinton (2003), Archbishop Desmond Tutu (2004), Nobel Peace Laureate Wangari Maathai of Kenya (2005), former South African President Thabo Mbeki (2006), and Liberian President Ellen Johnson-Sirleaf (2008).

Photograph by Jon Hrusa

▲ **HAPPY HILLARY:** U.S. Secretary of State Hillary Clinton smiles as Mandela welcomes her during a courtesy call at the Nelson Mandela Foundation in Johannesburg in August 2009. Speaking earlier in Pretoria, Clinton encouraged South Africa to use its clout to bolster reforms in Zimbabwe. She said closer ties would be built with South Africa following strains in the relationship under the Bush administration. Clinton and her husband, former U.S. President Bill Clinton, have long been personal friends of Mandela.

Photograph by Denis Farrell

Machel, a leading activist in the field of children's development in Africa, has been married to the presidents of two different African countries in one lifetime.

◀ **ELDER STATESMAN AND HIS FIRST LADY:** Nobel Peace Laureate Nelson Mandela and his wife, Graça Machel, attend the 2009 Nelson Mandela lecture in Johannesburg. Machel, a leading activist in the field of children's development in Africa, has been married to the presidents of two different African countries in one lifetime. The 2009 lecturer, Muhammad Yunus—founder of the Grameen Bank, which is helping roll back poverty in Bangladesh through microfinance—called on South Africa to become the first country to conquer poverty.

Photograph by Louise Gubb

▼ **FOLLOWING PAGES:** An old but wise Nelson Mandela surveys the stunningly beautiful Franschhoek Valley in the heart of the Cape wine lands. Mandela told this writer on many occasions how he valued the time he had to think while he was imprisoned. Here he seems to be back in a contemplative mood, reflecting on the long life that took him from a small village in the Transkei to the center of the world stage, from an angry revolutionary to a man of peace and compassion who transformed not only a nation but an era.

Photograph by Louise Gubb

PHOTOGRAPHY SOURCES

Names in parentheses indicate the original source of the photograph. Photographs not credited below were provided directly by the individual photographers who created them. Their names appear at the end of adjacent photo captions throughout the book. If no photographer's name appears at the end of a caption, the photographer is unknown.

AFRICA MEDIA ONLINE, JOHANNESBURG: *(All photographs from Africa Media Online were originally from Drum Social Histories.)* Pages 10, 27, 28–29, 33, 34, 35 (Mayibuye Centre), 36–37, 50, 52–53

THE ASSOCIATED PRESS: Pages 24–25, 41, 51, 58, 63, 66, 82 (Argus)

CORBIS: Pages 3, 39 (Reuters), 44–45 (2, Felicity Brian Literary Agency/Sygma), 49 (Reuters), 54 (Reuters), 88–89 (Saba), 90–91, 96–97 (Sygma), 101, 110–111 (Saba), 112–113 (Saba), 114–115 (Gallo), 116–117, 118–119 (Sygma), 120–121 (Saba), 124–125 (Saba), 133 (Saba), 134–135 (Saba), 136–137 (Saba), 138–139 (Saba), 140–141 (Saba), 142–143 (Saba), 143 (Sygma), 150–151, 156, 158–159, 160–161, 162–163, 164–165, 168–169, 170 (Sygma), 171 (Sygma), 172–173, 175 (Saba), 176–177 (Saba), 179 (Saba), 186, 188–189 (Reuters), 192–193 (Reuters), 194, 196–197 (Saba), 198–199 (Sygma), 200–201 (Sygma), 206–207 (Reuters), 208–209 (Sygma), 210 (Reuters), 211 (Saba), 216 (STR/epa), 218 (epa), 219 (Reuters)

GETTY IMAGES: Pages 4, 9, 26, 43 (Keystone), 92–93 (Redferns), 129 (Agence France-Presse), 184 (Media24/Gallo)

THE GRANGER COLLECTION: *(All photographs from the Granger Collection were originally from ullstein bild, Berlin.)* Pages 16, 46

LINK PICTURE LIBRARY, LONDON: *(All photographs from Link were originally from the University of the Western Cape—Robben Island Museum, Mayibuye Archives.)* Pages 25, 30, 38–39, 42, 46–47, 78–79, 80–81 (2)

CONTRIBUTORS

Produced and Directed by: David Elliot Cohen

Text by: John D. Battersby

Designed by: Peter Truskier and David Elliot Cohen

Production and Color Management by: Peter Truskier, Premedia Systems, Inc.

Copyedited by: Sherri Schultz

Intern: Colleen Mahoney

SPECIAL THANKS TO:

Lori Barra at Tonbo Designs and Michael Fragnito, Barbara Berger, Fred Pagan, and Elizabeth Mihaltse at Sterling Publishing. Also to our families... who didn't see much of us for a while.

REFERENCES

Carlin, John. *Playing the Enemy: Nelson Mandela and the Game That Made a Nation.* New York: Penguin, 2008.

Gregory, James. *Goodbye Bafana: Nelson Mandela, My Prisoner, My Friend.* London: Headline, 1995.

Joffe, Joel. *The State vs. Nelson Mandela: The Trial That Changed South Africa.* Oxford: Oneworld, 2007.

Lodge, Tom. *Mandela: A Critical Life.* New York: Oxford University Press, 2006.

Magubane, Peter. *Mandela: Man of the People.* Johannesburg, South Africa: Pan Macmillan, 2008.

Maharaj, Mac, ed. *Reflections in Prison.* Johannesburg, South Africa: Struik, 2002.

Mandela: The Authorized Portrait. Kansas City, MO: Andrews McMeel, 2006.

Mandela, Nelson. *An Illustrated Autobiography.* New York: Little Brown, 1994.

Nelson Mandela Foundation. *The Prisoner in the Garden: Opening Nelson Mandela's Prison Archive.* Johannesburg, South Africa: Penguin, 2005.

O'Malley, Padraig. *Shades of Difference: Mac Maharaj and the Struggle for South Africa.* New York: Viking, 2007.

Russell, Alec. *After Mandela: The Battle for the Soul of South Africa.* London: Hutchinson, 2009.

Sampson, Anthony. *Mandela: The Authorised Biography.* New York: Vintage, 1999.

Smith, Charlene. *Mandela: In Celebration of a Great Life.* Johannesburg, South Africa: Struik, 1999.

Sparks, Allister. *Tomorrow Is Another Country.* Johannesburg, South Africa: Struik, 1994.

Turnley, David. *Mandela! Struggle & Triumph.* New York: Harry N. Abrams, 2008.

Waldmeir, Patti. *Anatomy of a Miracle.* New York: Norton, 1997.

Zapiro. *The Mandela Files.* Lansdowne, South Africa: Double Storey, 2009.

In addition, the website of the African National Congress, www.anc.org.za, was an invaluable source of historical information and documents used in the preparation of this book.

AMANDLA NGAWETHU!